PRAISE FOR
THE CULTURE OF EMPOWERMENT

I appreciate having someone like Steve Backlund on our team. He is a true biblical leader in that he lives to bring out the best in others. I could safely say that some of the happiest people in our environment are the ones that work with the Backlunds, as both Steve and Wendy enable people to thrive. It is wonderful to see their insights and experiences put into a book. Now more people will have the language and the tools to be the kind of leader that Jesus modeled for us all. *The Culture of Empowerment* is both inspirational and practical, offering much encouragement and insight. I believe this book will have a powerful impact.

Bill Johnson
Bethel Church, Redding, CA
Author of *When Heaven Invades Earth* and *God is Good*

Steve Backlund is legendary in his ability to mentor and empower people. His new book, *The Culture of Empowerment*, reveals the heart and strategy for creating an environment of empowerment for those you lead. The timely wisdom and practical steps in this book make it a must-read for leaders of all kinds. I highly recommend it!

Kris Vallotton
Senior Associate Leader, Bethel Church, Redding, CA
Co-Founder of Bethel School of Supernatural Ministry
Author of eleven books, including *The Supernatural Ways of Royalty* and *Spirit Wars*

This book is written by the man who is surrounded by champions who will never forget the investment he's made in their lives. Year after year these champions hit new benchmarks of achievement and character. Steve Backlund is *THE* man who should write a book called *The Culture of Empowerment.* He is constantly doing exactly that. Study everything in this book and do it! Steve Backlund is a master teacher and example in developing people who become champions! I cannot recommend this book highly enough. Get it and do it, please!

Danny Silk
President of Loving on Purpose
Author of *Keep Your Love On, Culture of Honor,* and *Powerful and Free*

If I had to list the top five people who have influenced my leadership and helped me "get started," Steve Backlund is one of those. He is one of the most intentional, articulate, and diligent leaders I know. I'm excited to see how and what this book does to its readers. I know you will walk away with some keys and insights that will be helpful in your journey of life.

Eric Johnson
Senior Pastor of Bethel Redding
Author, *Christ in You* and *Momentum* (with Bill Johnson)

Steve Backlund is one of the most intentional men and leaders that I know. He is truly inspiring and carries a transformational message. Over the years, I have heard again and again how believed in, invested in, and empowered his teams feel, and I have always wanted to know what he does to create such powerful experiences. After reading this book, I feel as though I now know some of his tools and secrets. This book will transform the way you think of others, how you engage with people, and how you approach leadership. You will find powerful and practical keys to grow your favor and influence with others.

Candace Johnson
Senior Pastor of Bethel Redding

Steve Backlund is one of my favorite leaders and this is a book he has lived well before he wrote it. I have learned so much from watching him believe in his interns and ministry students more than they believe in themselves as he gives them opportunities to grow and stretch. As a result, it catalyzed them to take risks and go farther than they could have without those empowering beliefs. I have learned from his life how to have high-level beliefs about the people I lead—especially when I see their flaws and failures. This book gives us a window into the core values and skills needed for living a lifestyle of empowerment. Experience why our church calls Steve "an infuser of hope tsunamis," "a transformational architect," and "an impossibility catalyst."

Jim Baker
Senior Leader
Zion Christian Fellowship, Powell, OH
Author, *How Heaven Invades Your Finances*

Steve Backlund has changed my life! I have known Steve for the better part of a decade, I have hosted him in our church, and I have partnered with him in various expressions of ministry. I have rarely met a leader who carries such a powerful message and lives it out so well. This latest book by Steve and his co-authors presents the wisdom he has gained from decades of pastoring and combines his expertise as a premier "Beliefs Coach" to produce a powerful resource for seasoned and emerging leaders alike. This book should be required reading for anyone who is passionate about empowering others.

Michael Brodeur
Director of Pastor's Coach (PastorsCoach.com)
Author of *Destiny Finder* and *Revival Culture* (with Banning Liebscher)

STEVE BACKLUND

with PHIL BACKLUND
and Melissa Amato

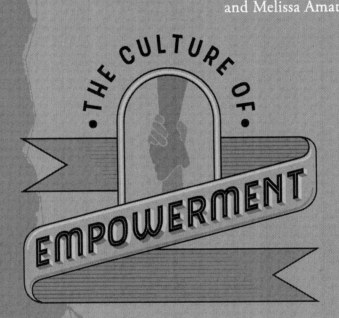

THE CULTURE OF

EMPOWERMENT

HOW TO
CHAMPION
PEOPLE

The Culture of Empowerment
© copyright 2016 Steve Backlund, Igniting Hope Ministries
www.ignitinghope.com

Cover design: Robert Schwendenmann (bobbyhere@gmail.com)
Interior layout and formatting: Robert Schwendenmann
Editors: Melissa Amato and Megan Cotton
Special thanks to: Jared Cullop, Julie Mustard, Daniel Newton, Dean Ras, and Benjamin Winkley
Thanks also to: Ahab Alhindi, Slindile Baloyi, Lauren DeTombe, Sarah Gerber, Ellie Goldberg, Julia Graham, Julie Heth, Rebecca Hill, Grace Lee, Emma Nainby, Chris Pollasch, MJ Robinson
Empowerment Assessment developers: Samuel Verbi and Benjamin Winkley (www.eidoresearch.com)

ISBN-13: 978-0-9863094-6-5

THE CULTURE OF EMPOWERMENT

Steve Backlund

with Phil Backlund and Melissa Amato

This book is dedicated to the Bethel School of Supernatural Ministry mentors. Your investment in the school's Third Year students is shaping history.
Thank you for all you do.

CONTENTS

ABOUT THE AUTHORS

STEVE BACKLUND was a senior pastor for seventeen years before joining the team at Bethel Church in Redding, CA in 2008. Steve is a leader developer, joy activist, a revivalist teacher, a hope igniter, and as Senior Associate Director, is a key part of the Global Legacy leadership team at Bethel Church. He and his wife Wendy founded Igniting Hope Ministries and they travel extensively throughout the world encouraging churches and leaders. They have authored many books and enjoy their seven grandchildren.

PHIL BACKLUND received his Bachelor's degree in Business Administration and Master's degree in Speech Communication from Humboldt State University, and he earned his PhD in Speech Communication from the University of Denver. He had an academic position at the University of Alaska in Fairbanks, taught at Utica College, and recently retired as a Professor of Communication Studies at Central Washington University. Phil loves teaching, and firmly believes that as a teacher, one of the most important gifts he can give his students is the ability to communicate effectively in public, small group, interpersonal, and intercultural contexts. He values building international goodwill, and has worked and taught in Hong Kong, Macau, Tanzania, South Sudan, and Pakistan. Phil and his wife, Judy, have three children – Shane, Ryan, and Matthew – and are involved in their community, serving on a number of boards over the years. Family is important to Phil, and he very much enjoys his wonderful children and grandchildren. He is very pleased to be involved with this project with his brother Steve.

MELISSA AMATO has worked in a variety of career fields, including business, medicine, performing arts, and education. She is a Third Year graduate of BSSM where she interned for Steve Backlund, then worked in Global Legacy as his assistant, and is now the BSSM Third Year Intern and Mentor Pastor. Melissa is ordained by Bethel Church and frequently travels, sharing her heart for intimacy and encounters with God at churches throughout the world. She is passionate about people experiencing God's love, hope, peace, and joy and living the abundant life Jesus paid for.

FOREWORD

By Wendy Backlund

I do not know of anyone better qualified to write a book on empowerment. My husband, Steve, is the most empowering leader I have ever met. I have personally benefited from his gift to not only empower those around him, but to champion them. I fully believe that without him (and Jesus of course), I would never have fully realized my potential as a writer, speaker, and leader. Steve believed in me when I could not believe in myself. As he focused on my strengths and gifts, it gave me courage and a reason to work on my weaknesses.

The Culture of Empowerment is a book the world has been waiting for. We are now in a season for the Church and every organization to equip, champion, and release the people God has given them. In this book, Steve shares how he has created a culture where everyone feels empowered and safe. He has a unique ability to cause people to mature through vision and hope rather than guilt or performance. And, as a bonus, you will glean from Steve's brother Phil, who gives great insights from his academic training, life experience, and years of being a college professor. Phil is also a man I highly respect, and I've gleaned wisdom as I've watched him in both his academics and in how he empowered his three sons into success.

Prepare yourself to be challenged to see people differently, which is the main ingredient of an empowering culture. The insights and strategies of this book will take your beliefs and leadership to a whole new level.

INTRODUCTION

I am thrilled to finally release *The Culture of Empowerment*. It has been years in the making, but the wait has allowed us to add significant additional material (especially the contributions of my brother Phil who has a PhD in Communications and has been a college professor for decades).

I have probably learned the most important truths about empowerment from my 38 years of marriage with Wendy. She is wired very differently than me, and I initially tried to motivate her through guilt and manipulation. This resulted from my bad beliefs that created disempowering attitudes and words, which I projected onto her. I am glad to report this method of trying to influence my wife did not work, and she didn't respond well (which is probably no surprise to you).

I finally gave up trying to control Wendy through negativity, and instead I started to believe in her more than she believed in herself. This belief from me was catalytic in her blossoming as a person and influencer. I took this experience with Wendy and began to similarly believe in the people around me in greater ways. I was amazed at what I saw happen. Their hope levels began to grow and I realized this was the missing ingredient to see great transformation in people.

My friend Danny Silk has written a great book called *Keep Your Love On*. This book you are now reading could have aptly been titled *Keep Your Beliefs On*. Even though this manuscript is filled with diverse truths on the topic of empowerment, the foundation of our teaching is to develop great beliefs about the people in your life and in those you lead. God sets the example for us by empowering us more than we think we should be empowered, and this forms the basis for how we are to treat people under our influence.

This writing will reveal a solid biblical basis for living a lifestyle of empowerment. I believe after you read this book, you will find it inconceivable to believe you should try to control people through anger and/or the fear of punishment. I believe you will be aroused in your spirit to truly inspire others to greater heights through powerful beliefs and organizational structures that are life-giving to them (and not simply have organizational systems that benefit the leaders).

Again, I am thankful for my brother Phil who has given us a wealth of insight on such topics as listening, public speaking, conflict resolution, and more. His academic perspective and life experiences brought so much strength to me in this writing. Also, I am thankful for my former personal assistant Melissa Amato, who has also helped me so much in determining the content of the book and has written a few sections herself. My wife, Wendy Backlund, contributed a chapter on empowering yourself. I am indebted to her and the many others who have spent hours with me on this book.

My desire is that everyone will benefit by *The Culture of Empowerment*, especially those who lead or mentor people. Be blessed as you read.

Steve Backlund

EMPOWERMENT ASSESSMENT

We reccommend taking the Empowerment Assessment before you begin this book.

To best assess your current level of empowerment, log on to:

http://ignitinghope.com/empowerment-assessment

After completing the online assessment, record your score and the date below.

Initial Score: Date:

Once you have completed this book and implement truths that are highlighted to you, use the link above to take the Empowerment Assessment again. We recommend you track your progress on your journey of growing in the culture of empowerment. We bless you in this process, and we believe in you!

WHAT IS EMPOWERMENT?

My goal is not to build a big church, but to build big people.
Bill Johnson

"What am I doing here?" I wondered as I sat in a room full of church elders. I was an apprentice leader who was invited to sit in on leadership meetings to learn from these more seasoned leaders. I felt insecure and out of place. Why did Pastor Fred (our senior leader) want me to be a part of this group? I had not yet even turned twenty-five years old. It just didn't make sense.

"I really don't belong here," I thought to myself. Just then I heard Fred's voice jolting me back to reality. He asked, "Steve, what is your opinion on the situation we are discussing?"

Inside my head I was asking: "What?! Why is he asking me?! There is well over a one hundred years of ministry experience in the room, and he is asking what I think? Why would he do that?"

Pastor Fred Muster not only asked me to join leadership meetings, but he also opened up preaching opportunities at other churches before I thought I was ready. He trained me how to teach and preach, and then sent me out when I still felt unsure about it. I will never forget that season of my life. It was an interesting mixture of fear and excitement.

Fred did what all great leaders do. They inspire people, give them opportunities, and provide support as needed. As a young leader, I was infused with a passion by Fred and others who caused me to believe I could change the world because I had something significant to contribute. They saw good things in me that I couldn't see in myself, and their endorsement of me opened doors that I could not open for myself. Fred was the first of many who did so. I was changed by his influence, and I have dedicated myself to do the same for others in every season of my life.

Have you ever been championed by someone? You have likely had times when people believed in you more than you believed in yourself and told you, "YOU CAN DO IT!" Their belief in you became a rock to stand on against the waves of insecurity, doubt, and fear in your mind. They were willing to allow you to try something challenging and new under their mentorship, and it caused you to find out there was more in you than you thought.

You may not realize it, but you were *empowered* by these people. The Oxford Dictionary definition of *empower* is: 1) Give (someone) the authority or power to do something; 2) Make (someone) stronger and more confident. These definitions combine three of the key components of empowerment: inspiration, opportunity, and backing.

Inspiration – Great influencers know how to inspire people to do what they never thought they could do. They make others feel stronger and more confident. Just like great sport coaches, empowering leaders inspire their "teams" to do more than they thought was possible.

Opportunity – Empowering people constantly look for ways to include others so they can grow in their gifts and make a significant difference. Like the masters of old, strong leaders give "apprentices" opportunity to grow under their mentorship. They realize one of their most important privileges and responsibilities is to pass on what they know to the next generation.

Backing – Those who empower "send" people into assignments with training and support, taking the responsibility for what happens through these sent ones. There is also an anointing (impartation) from the leader that the one being empowered can access to do more than they imagined. Jesus backed the disciples in Luke 10, and they were amazed that even the demons were subject to them.

The great leaders of the world not only empower but also create an empowering culture. Jesus brought twelve ordinary men into His "culture" for three years and they changed the world. David had 400 "3D" people come to him: "And everyone *who was* in **distress**, everyone *who was* in **debt**, and everyone *who was* **discontented** gathered to him. So he became captain over them" (1 Samuel 22:2). This motley crew became the Mighty Men of 2 Samuel 23 who did unbelievable exploits. Both Jesus and David championed people beyond what they thought they were capable of.

THAT THEY MIGHT BE WITH HIM

One of God's greatest methods to reach the planet with the gospel and to change the world is by mentoring a team of people. Robert E. Coleman's book *The Master Plan of Evangelism* highlights Jesus' priority to invest in twelve men for three years. "And He went up on the mountain and called to *Him* those He Himself wanted. And they came to Him. *Then He appointed twelve, that they might be with Him* and that He might send them out to preach" (Mark 3:13-14). He appointed them first to be "with Him." Let that sink in. Jesus ministered to the many, but He resolutely poured into a few.

What were the results of this? It was world shaking! It was transformational for the disciples. Their lives far exceeded what was the norm for people like them. "Now when they (the educated religious leaders of their day) saw the boldness of Peter and John, and perceived that they were uneducated and untrained men, they marveled. *And they realized that they had been with Jesus*" (Acts 4:13).

A true culture of empowerment:
- Prioritizes relationships and heart connections
- Causes transformation in lives that others will marvel at
- Creates boldness (confidence) in those being empowered

THE SAME CULTURE THAT CREATED A JUDAS ALSO PRODUCED ELEVEN WORLD CHANGERS

It would be an understatement to say Jesus was a great leader, but even He had a "failure" under Him in Judas (who ultimately betrayed Jesus). Empowering leaders will at times have people under their leadership who will disappoint them, but these leaders will continue to believe in the people they have around them. They know that if they let the fear of betrayal or fear of problems dominate their thinking, then they will lose the edge on their leadership to truly empower others.

> *Remember this:* if our goal is to prevent a Judas from manifesting in our midst, we will probably never have eleven world changers.

Through His empowering people, Jesus set an example for us. He revealed the Father's heart in doing so. The Father has empowered us from the beginning. It is His nature to partner with our strategies to "Be fruitful and multiply; fill the earth and subdue it" (Genesis 1:28). As we understand this heart of the Father more clearly from Scripture, we will recognize our equipping, endorsing, and giving opportunities of influence to others is simply our following the very heart of God.

The rest of this chapter shares much of the biblical foundation for being an empowering person and for creating a culture of empowerment around us.

GOD SET THE EXAMPLE FOR US BY EMPOWERING US

As we study Scripture, it is clear that God empowers and commissions people to accomplish divine purposes on earth. He has put seemingly unlimited potential in us for advancement in our lives and in worldwide events. The following biblical passages help us see God's heart in this.

In the beginning, God empowered mankind – "Then God said, 'Let Us make man in Our image, according to Our likeness; let them have dominion over the fish of the sea, over the birds of the air, and over the cattle, over all the earth and over every creeping thing that creeps on the earth.' So God created man in His *own* image; in the image of God He created him; male and female He created them. Then God blessed them, and God said to them, *'Be fruitful and multiply; fill the earth and subdue it*; have dominion over the fish of the sea, over the birds of the air, and over every living thing that moves on the earth'" (Genesis 1:26-28). **Jesus came to empower us into life** – "The thief does not come except to steal, and to kill, and to destroy. I have come that they may have life, and that they may have *it* more abundantly" (John 10:10). Jesus released us from limitation and disempowerment, and now we have the privilege of experiencing this by faith more and more in our lives.

Christ's empowerment far surpasses sin's disempowerment – "For if by the one man's offense death reigned through the one, much more those who receive abundance of grace and of the gift of righteousness will reign in life through the One, Jesus Christ" (Romans 5:17). This "reigning in life" comes to those who receive the abundance of grace (which is the empowerment do God's will) and the gift of righteousness (believing we are in right standing with God based on what Jesus has done).

Jesus took the keys of authority on earth from the devil and has given them to us – "And I will give you the keys of the Kingdom of heaven, and whatever you bind on earth will be bound in heaven, and whatever you loose on earth will be loosed in heaven" (Matthew 16:19). "Having disarmed principalities and powers, He made a public spectacle of them, triumphing over them in it" (Colossians 2:15).

Believing and confessing empower us to experience what Jesus' won for us – "That if you confess with your mouth the Lord Jesus and believe in your heart that God has raised Him from the dead, you will be saved. For with the heart one believes unto righteousness, and with the mouth confession is made unto salvation" (Romans 10:9-10). Empowerment is not automatic in our lives, but it is to be accessed by faith and by having our words come into agreement with what God has done and who He says we are.

Holy Spirit empowers us with an inner compulsion to impact others with a supernatural edge on our lives – "But you shall receive power when the Holy Spirit has come upon you; and you shall be witnesses to Me in Jerusalem, and in all Judea and Samaria, and to the end of the earth" (Acts 1:8).

Holy Spirit empowers us to do greater things than even Jesus did – "Most assuredly, I say to you, he who believes in Me, the works that I do he will do also; and greater *works* than these he will do, because I go to My Father. And whatever you ask in My name, that I will do, that the Father may be glorified in the Son. If you ask anything in My name, I will do *it*" (John 14:12-14). Even though none of us are fully walking in what Jesus is describing here, this is an incredible invitation to expand our expectations of what God's empowerment can mean for our lives.

Humility attracts empowerment – "God resists the proud, but gives grace to the humble. Therefore humble yourselves under the mighty hand of God, that He may exalt you in due time" (1 Peter 5:5). Being humble does not mean you walk in insecurity or lack confidence, but it is a lifestyle of knowing you need God and other people to accomplish your assignments in life.

Leaders are to primarily equip (empower) people to do the work of ministry – "And He Himself gave some *to* be apostles, some prophets, some evangelists, and some pastors and teachers, for the equipping of the saints for the work of ministry, for the edifying of the body of Christ" (Ephesians 4:11-12). Even though we realize everyone is to empower others in relationships, it is noteworthy that one of the main roles of Christian leadership is to train and release others to do influential things.

God empowers our work in the Kingdom – "I also labor, striving according to His working which works in me mightily" (Colossians 1:29). "I labored more abundantly than they all, yet not I, but the grace of God *which was* with me" (1 Corinthians 15:10). We are not called to work "for God," but we have the privilege of working "with God" and His empowering grace. The supernatural is not something reserved for miracles and healings, but it is to be a reality in all we do.

God's empowerment takes all limitations off of our lives – "Now to Him who is able to do exceedingly abundantly above all that we ask or think, according to the power that works in us" (Ephesians 3:20). God can do so much more than we can think of or imagine, and with Him all things are possible (Matthew 19:26).

Being born again is the beginning point of true empowerment – "Jesus answered and said to him, 'Most assuredly, I say to you, unless one is born again, he cannot see the Kingdom of God.' Nicodemus said to Him, 'How can a man be born when he is old? Can he enter a second time into his mother's womb and be born?' Jesus answered, 'Most assuredly, I say to you, unless one is born of water and the Spirit, he cannot enter the Kingdom of God. That which is born of the flesh is flesh, and that which is born of the Spirit is spirit'" (John 3:3-6). When there is decline in families and nations, God's answer is a new wave of conversions (people being born again).

HERE ARE MORE BIBLICAL EXAMPLES OF GOD'S HEART TO SEE US EMPOWERED:

"But He answered and said to them, 'You give them something to eat'" (Mark 6:37) – Jesus did not feed the 5,000, the disciples did. God loves to empower and multiply what we give Him to supernaturally meet the needs around us.

"Brother Saul, ... receive your sight and be filled with the Holy Spirit" (Acts 9:17) – Ananias was empowered by God to bring freedom to Saul. It is important to note that Jesus and the Apostles (in the Gospels and Acts) *spoke* to people and things to bring healing, resurrection, calm weather, etc. They did not pray and ask the Heavenly Father to do these things. They had the revelation they were God's delegated authority, empowered to see and release His will to be done on earth as it is heaven.

"Prophesy to these bones" (Ezekiel 37:4) – After Ezekiel prophesied to the dry bones, they became "an exceedingly great army" (Ezekiel 37:10). God did not say to Ezekiel, "Step aside and watch Me prophesy to these dry bones." God has chosen to partner with people who have enough hope to speak life into situations. He has empowered us to determine how much change there will be around us.

"Looking for and hastening the coming of the day of God" (2 Peter 3:12) – God has even empowered us to impact the timing of His plans. Mary hastened the timing of when Jesus started doing miracles (John 2:1-11). Abraham had a New Covenant experience in the Old Covenant when his beliefs actually transformed his identity before God (Genesis 15:6). This verse suggests that we can even impact events like the return of Christ.

"So the Lord relented from the harm which He said He would do to His people" (Exodus 32:14) – Moses changed God's mind through his intercession for the people he led. We too are empowered to divert negative consequences directed at people and nations.

"Go home to your friends, and tell them what great things the Lord has done for you" (Mark 5:19) – Once he was delivered, the demon-possessed man of the Gadarenes was immediately empowered by Jesus to witness to his friends.

"The Lord appointed seventy others also, and sent them two by two" (Luke 10:1) – In Luke 9, Jesus sent and empowered the twelve to proclaim and demonstrate the Kingdom. After they returned, they manifested immaturity by arguing with each other, wanting to forbid someone from preaching who was not in their group, and wanting to call fire down from heaven on a village that had rejected Jesus. Even though the disciples demonstrated these dysfunctional behaviors, Jesus empowered even more of them in Luke 10 to bring the Kingdom to the people around them.

CONCLUSION

God's original purpose for mankind was to see them empowered. Sin short-circuited this plan, but God had a remedy in Jesus to restore us to all things that were lost, including our empowerment. Before Jesus, it was impossible to live a life pleasing to God, but our Father pursued relationship with us so we could truly live.

The New Testament is a revelation of God's grace toward us. Grace not only puts us in right standing with the Father, but it literally empowers us to do God's will. We are infused with supernatural power to do what the Bible commands. God does not command us to do something that He does not also give us the power to do. He has literally created a culture of empowerment for us to blossom in.

If we are not an empowering person, there will be a tendency to resort to such methods as control, manipulation, and a fear of punishment in order to motivate those in our lives. Sometimes we as Christians use these negative tools because we misunderstand the heart and ways of God.

The heavenly example God gives us is our prototype for our influence and leadership. God believes in us more than we believe in ourselves. He has empowering beliefs about us. Our next chapter will share about these beliefs in specific ways, and we will see it is impossible to create a culture of empowerment without embracing these beliefs ourselves.

WHAT WE ARE NOT SAYING

- We are not saying we should ignore character flaws in people.
- We are not saying everyone should be empowered equally.
- We are not saying obedience is unimportant in the Christian life.

DECLARATIONS

- Like Jesus, I create a culture of empowerment around me where people thrive.
- I inspire people, give them opportunities, and I support them in what they do.
- I have a strong biblical foundation for creating a culture of empowerment.

EMPOWERING BELIEFS

*We get saved because we believe **in** Jesus, but we will have supernatural influence because we believe **like** Jesus.*

Steve Backlund

I remember whining once to the Lord about the people in my ministry. "Lord, if I had better people in my church, then I could really do something. I am trying to fly like an eagle, but I am landlocked with all these prairie chickens. I am a victim of the people I am trying to lead." Even though this felt true about them, it was not the truth.

I have learned that lies feel very real when they stay in the darkness of our thinking, but they become laughable when they are brought out into the light of language and words. When I verbalized my beliefs about being a victim of my people, I realized it was more a reflection of my leadership than anything they were doing. I began to realize I was believing something wrong that was blocking God's best for my people and me.

The Kingdom of God is not moved forward by good conduct, but by good beliefs (see Galatians 3:1-5). The most important question of the hour is not, "Lord, what should I do?" but it is, "Lord, what should I believe? What should I renew my mind with about You, about myself, about others, and about my circumstances?" We certainly recognize how people's actions and choices will impact the quality of their lives, but it is vital to understand that good beliefs are the key to upgrading people's conduct.

This is a chapter that addresses our beliefs about the people in our lives. The foundation for having good beliefs about others is to have good beliefs about ourselves. Jesus said, "Love your neighbor as you love yourself" (Mark 12:31). How we feel about ourselves will most likely be how we will feel about others. We will say more about this later. Jesus had incredible beliefs about His disciples. He believed if they spent time with Him and were filled with the Holy Spirit, they would be transformed and change the world.

One of the greatest things leaders can do is to believe in the people they lead. People generally rise to the level of the beliefs of the important people in their lives, but we also know it can be challenging to keep believing in people – especially after we begin to see their shortcomings.

It is said, "Familiarity breeds contempt." This negative tendency results from a common pattern in relationships:
- First, we get excited about who we believe a person is.
- Second, we become disappointed when we start seeing flaws in him or her.
- Third, we base our future beliefs about the person from his or her past experience rather than who God says he or she is.

Catalytic leaders know how to break this cycle – and they do so without being gullible and unwise in relationships. Instead of developing their beliefs about people from their past, they see people through God's eyes. This causes the third step of the relationship pattern above to change to growth. Thus the common pattern in relationships becomes: 1) Excitement, 2) Disappointment, and 3) Growth.

It is impossible to be an empowering person without having empowering beliefs about the people in our lives. We can create an empowering culture without first addressing our thinking about others. This book is written to help us be the kind of leader who believes in others at a high level.

Romans 12:2 says, "Be transformed by the renewing of your mind." Whatever truths or lies we renew our mind with now, will later dominate our future experience. The empowering leader *thinks on purpose* about the people in his or her life.

God doesn't ask us to do something we can't do, so we know there's grace available to think more highly about the people around us. The following verse reveals the kinds of thoughts high-level thinkers embrace: "Finally, brethren, whatever things *are* true, whatever things *are* noble, whatever things *are* just, whatever things *are* pure, whatever things *are* lovely, whatever things *are* of good report, if *there is* any virtue and if *there is* anything praiseworthy – meditate on these things" (Philippians 4:8).

Many Christians emphasize a lifestyle of "spiritual warfare" to combat the ploys of the devil, but it is important to understand that the highest level of spiritual warfare is to take "every thought into captivity." It is the decision to think and see through God's perspective about people, circumstances, and ourselves. "For the weapons of our warfare *are* not carnal but mighty in God for pulling down strongholds, casting down arguments and every high thing that exalts itself against the knowledge of God, bringing every thought into captivity to the obedience of Christ" (2 Corinthians 10:4-5).

Many think that 2 Corinthians 10:4-5 is talking about pulling down strongholds of the devil, but it is actually referring to addressing our own belief systems. Certainly we don't discount the influence of the devil, but the greatest strongholds blocking the purposes of God are in our own minds, not something the devil is doing. Even the individual pieces of the armor of God in Ephesians 6 cannot be put on without believing truths related to each of these pieces.

One of the biggest "spiritual warfare" battles a person will face is to maintain high beliefs about the people in his or her life. It truly can be a mental warfare to resist the temptation of creating identity beliefs from people's past experience instead of from God's Word.

How then do we know if we have good beliefs about people? **I believe our hope level for people is a main indicator of whether we are believing lies or truth about them.** We will know the renewing of the mind is working because our hope is increasing (Hebrews 10:23; Romans 15:13). Decreased hope for people is a fruit of believing lies instead of believing truth.

The empowering person's worldview will indeed be much more hope-filled than the non-empowering person's. This is especially true for Christians who embrace the power of the new birth that happens when they put their faith in Jesus. "Therefore, if anyone *is* in Christ, *he is* a new creation; old things have passed away; behold, all things have become new" (2 Corinthians 5:17). These new creation beliefs cause a dramatic rise in hope about ourselves and will also cause us to see others at a higher level.

How do we keep powerful beliefs about the people we lead? Do we try to pump up positive thoughts for them, or is there a better way? There is a better way indeed. It is to believe truth about them. Jesus said, "The truth will make you free" (John 8:32). Freedom (empowerment) comes when we believe what God says rather than believing what the past or our feelings say.

What does God say about people? What truths will shape our beliefs and be catalytic in creating a culture of empowerment around us?

15 POWERFUL BELIEFS

Here are fifteen biblical beliefs that will radically impact your thinking about others and then ultimately radically impact the people in your life:

1. **Vision Beliefs About Others** – "Brethren, I do not count myself to have apprehended; but one thing *I do*, forgetting those things which are behind and reaching forward to those things which are ahead" (Philippians 3:13). The people in our lives have "things" to reach forward to. Every person is significant in God and has an important assignment from Him. Our vision for the future gives us purpose for the present. It means we are being prepared for something bigger (greater influence) in the days ahead. As we recognize this about those we are leading, we will find ourselves saying things like, "Where you are going, you can't take *that* with you" (whether it be a tendency, attitude, or something else). We will focus on training them to be ready for this greater opportunity, instead of only trying to get them to be a good employee, a good Christian, or less of a problem to us.

2. **Hope Beliefs About Others** – "Let us hold fast the confession of *our* hope without wavering, for He who promised *is* faithful. And let us consider one another in order to stir up love and good works, not forsaking the assembling of ourselves together, as *is* the manner of some, but exhorting *one another,* and so much the more as you see the Day approaching" (Hebrews 10:23-25). We are told not to let go of our confession of hope. **This directive is linked to the relationships in our lives** – "consider one another," "assembling together," and "exhorting one another." "Exhorting" is translated as "encourage" in some Bible versions. Verse 25 tells us we are to increase encouragement as we "see the Day approaching." Instead of becoming more cynical as we grow

older, we are to become more hopeful of the good things in people around us. We are to believe they are one encouragement away from a tipping point in their lives – and we won't encourage those we are hopeless about. It is important to know this: Our hopelessness for people we lead is usually a bigger problem than what the people are doing.

3. **Love and Compassion Beliefs About Others** – "Then Jesus went about … healing every sickness and every disease among the people. But when He saw the multitudes, He was moved with compassion for them, because they were weary and scattered, like sheep having no shepherd" (Matthew 9:35-36). Compassion and true concern for people is foundational to influence. We are not simply to get things done for people or through people, but we are called to emotionally connect with the dreams and needs of those in our lives. "For in Christ Jesus neither circumcision nor uncircumcision avails anything, but faith working through love" (Galatians 5:7). Outward accomplishments are meaningless without it. In fact, 1 Corinthians 13 says we are "nothing" if relational love does not manifest through us, even if we are doing supernatural exploits. This "love chapter" of the Bible is about how we interact with people, and one of the highest ways we interact with them is what we believe about them. "[Love] believes all things, hopes all things" (1 Corinthians 13:7).

4. **Solution Beliefs About Others** – "No temptation has overtaken you except such as is common to man; but God *is* faithful, who will not allow you to be tempted beyond what you are able, but with the temptation will also make the way of escape, that you may be able to bear *it*" (1 Corinthians 10:13). This is one of the biggest hope verses in the Bible. It is an anchor verse to set others and us free from hopelessness. Two great truths are revealed that will radically upgrade our beliefs about the people we influence: 1) They will not face anything God has not equipped them to overcome, and 2) There is *always* "the way of escape" from where they are and into where they need to be. Say this out loud: "THERE IS ALWAYS A SOLUTION!" The people in our lives have a pathway to get out of crisis/dysfunction and a way to get into dreams/radical influence. This creates hope for them, which is a catalytic force for their empowerment.

5. **Encouragement Beliefs About Others** – "Say to those *who are* fearful-hearted, 'Be strong, do not fear! Behold, your God will come *with* vengeance, *with* the recompense of God; He will come and save you.' Then the eyes of the blind shall be opened, And the ears of the deaf shall be unstopped …"

(Isaiah 35:4-5). A well-timed encouragement from a person who believes his or her words are powerful can set off a chain reaction of supernaturally infused events.

6. **Prophetic Beliefs About Others** – "As it is written, 'I have made you a father of many nations' in the presence of Him whom he believed – God, who gives life to the dead and calls those things which do not exist as though they did" (Romans 4:17). God called Abraham by his future and invited Abraham to come into agreement with his future. Similarly, the angel unlocked Gideon's destiny by calling him by his future – "The Lord is with you, you mighty man of valor!" (Judges 6:12). Gideon, at the time, was certainly not living in a mighty man of valor experience, but his past didn't define who he was. Empowering leaders become like the angel in the lives of the "Gideons" who are all around them. They learn how to not lock the people they lead into their past. They see them prophetically.

7. **"Benefit of the Doubt" Beliefs About Others** – "Now John answered and said, 'Master, we saw someone casting out demons in Your name, and we forbade him because he does not follow with us.' But Jesus said to him, 'Do not forbid *him*, for he who is not against us is on our side'" (Luke 9:49-50). "The first *one* to plead his cause *seems* right, until his neighbor comes and examines him" (Proverbs 18:17). One way to decrease our empowerment of others is by jumping to negative conclusions about them – whether it is hearsay information we hear or a judgment we have about their motives. We tend to judge ourselves by our motives and others by their actions. It will serve us well in life and leadership if we give people the benefit of doubt and ask good questions before making a conclusion that might not be true.

8. **Association Beliefs About Others** – "Now when they saw the boldness of Peter and John, and perceived that they were uneducated and untrained men, they marveled. And they realized that they had been with Jesus" (Acts 4:13). A culture of empowerment has the potential of bringing a marvelous upgrade to the people who associate with it. The disciples astounded the elite people of their day because of their having "been with Jesus." Catalytic influencers will develop the belief system that it is impossible for people not to be changed when they associate with them.

9. **"Faith Comes by Hearing" Beliefs About Others** – "So then faith *comes* by hearing, and hearing by the Word of God" (Romans 10:17). If people are going to live at a higher level, they must believe at a higher level. If they

are going to believe at a higher level, they must hear truth at a higher level. Empowering leaders know speaking God's promises will increase the faith of the people in their lives. There is no such thing as a strong, silent-type leader.

10. **Forgiveness Beliefs About Others** – "Then Jesus said, 'Father, forgive them, for they do not know what they do'" (Luke 23:34). Jesus spoke forgiveness on the cross. Stephen did the same in Acts 7:59 when he was being stoned. Their forgiveness created an open Heaven over others to become saved (the 3,000 in Acts 2 and Saul of Tarsus in Acts 9). Our intentional forgiveness is a mighty spiritual weapon, which increases the likelihood of advancement and breakthrough in the lives of those we influence.

11. **Restoration Beliefs About Others** – "Brethren, if a man is overtaken in any trespass, you who *are* spiritual restore such a one in a spirit of gentleness, considering yourself lest you also be tempted" (Galatians 6:1). Empowering leaders see beyond people's failures and sins, and see who they really are. They have a heart and skill set that restores people back to wholeness and influence. They believe that under their leadership, people regularly get restored to their original design and purpose.

12. **Saint Beliefs About Others** – "Therefore, from now on, we regard no one according to the flesh … Therefore, if anyone *is* in Christ, *he is* a new creation; old things have passed away; behold, all things have become new … For He made Him who knew no sin *to be* sin for us, that we might become the righteousness of God in Him" (1 Corinthians 5:16-21). The Christians we are leading are saints, not sinners. We are not to regard them "according to the flesh." If we believe those in our life are sinners (prone to sin), then our beliefs about them will be less empowering. If we believe they are saints (prone to do right), then these positive beliefs will create empowerment for them.

13. **Testimony Beliefs About Others** – "For the testimony of Jesus is the spirit of prophecy" (Revelation 19:10). Somebody else has overcome the same situations that those around us are facing. As we focus on and share the testimonies of these victories, our hope of victory for ourselves and those we influence increases. This hope ultimately brings greater empowerment in our relationships.

14. **"Nothing is impossible" Beliefs About Others** – "So He asked his father, 'How long has this been happening to him?' And he said, 'From childhood.

And often he has thrown him both into the fire and into the water to destroy him. But if You can do anything, have compassion on us and help us.' Jesus said to him, 'If you can believe, all things *are* possible to him who believes.' Immediately the father of the child cried out and said with tears, 'Lord, I believe; help my unbelief!'" (Mark 9:21-24). The boy's healing and deliverance was not dependent on God's willingness (He's willing), but the father's beliefs had a lot to do with whether the son would be empowered into freedom. The father "got it" and asked for divine help in believing for a "nothing is impossible" belief system. Our beliefs in a supernatural empowerment to freedom for those we influence will have a bigger influence than we might think.

15. **"Golden Rule" Beliefs About Others** – "And just as you want men to do to you, you also do to them likewise" (Luke 6:31). How do you want others to treat you? How do you want leaders to think about you? How do you want the influencers in your life to treat you? Do this for others, and you will most likely be a very empowering leader.

The above beliefs are not just about the people in our lives, but they are also how God sees us. We suggest you take each of these beliefs and meditate on them as the way God believes in you. We cannot consistently do what we don't believe we are, so renewing our minds with these truths will empower us to do what we never thought we could do.

LEADING NON-CHRISTIANS

The basis for much of what we have said in this chapter is rooted in a person's identity in Christ. But what if we are leading people who have not professed faith in Christ? Should we still have high-level beliefs about them?

I believe the answer to this question is YES! Remember, people in general will rise to the level of the beliefs of important people in their lives. One good example of this is Daniel. He was in relationship with an ungodly king named Nebuchadnezzar. Daniel's love and believing the best for this king was instrumental in helping him personally, and it caused Nebuchadnezzar to have a powerful experience with God (Daniel 4:19-37). We too can increase our positive influence on all the people in our lives by having faith-filled beliefs about them.

CLOSING THOUGHTS

Our Heavenly Father has greatly empowered us. And as we accurately represent Him to other people, we will create a culture of empowerment around us. Because God believes in us more than we believe in ourselves, we are to believe in others more than they believe in themselves.

Truly, how we experience God will be a huge factor in how people experience us. Another way of saying this is: The attitude we have toward ourselves will be the attitude we have toward other people. Remember these words, "You shall love your neighbor as yourself." If we love ourselves, we will tend to love others. If we hate ourselves, we will be more prone to hate others. If we don't believe God wants to empower us, then we won't have faith to empower others. How we believe God treats us will be the basis for how we treat others.

It is vital to believe God desires to empower us. He has not made us slaves or pawns in the game of life, but we are friends and co-laborers with Him. If we are not convinced we are empowered, it will be difficult to empower others.

WHAT WE ARE NOT SAYING

- We are not saying we can only influence the people we have an official leadership role with.
- We are not saying empowering people will overlook character flaws in those they influence.
- We are not saying that introverts or quieter people cannot be strong leaders.

DECLARATIONS

- I believe in the people I lead more than they believe in themselves.
- I have an unusual ability to maintain high beliefs about the people in my life.
- I am full of hope for people.

God has not called us to be realistic. He has called us to be supernatural.

Wendy Backlund

INTRODUCTION FROM STEVE

My wife Wendy was my training ground on how to learn to empower others. She is completely opposite from me in personality and in how she is motivated. In the first years of our marriage, I tried to conform her into my own image by motivating her with guilt and manipulation. (Ha ha. You can imagine how that worked out.) When I saw this only hindered our relationship and caused her to shut down, I determined I would believe in her and love her unconditionally. It was one of the best decisions I've ever made in my life.

Wendy's transformation has been spectacular. She used to be very shy and timid (wanting to hide in the background). Now she is one of the strongest influencers I know, with a large following of people wanting what she has. I realize there were other factors for this change besides my empowering her, but when I saw the change in her, it ignited me to bring this change to others.

Enjoy Wendy's perspective on empowering yourself. It has some wonderful nuggets, and it is a good complement to what is in the rest of this book.

I f we want to be an empowering person, it is a good idea to begin by empowering ourselves. An empowered and victorious life results largely from having empowering beliefs about ourselves. Despite common belief, other people and circumstances are not our problem. Christ was one of the most empowered people on the planet because of what He believed about Himself. He faced some incredibly challenging circumstances, but He never took on a victim mentality. He chose to stay above His circumstances and knew that He was powerful. Even when He, a fully empowered, all-powerful person, went to the cross for us, He didn't see Himself as a victim of His circumstances or have a "poor Me" attitude – He chose to go to the cross.

Truly empowered people have overcome seeing themselves as victims. They understand that people and circumstances aren't holding them back. And although many use their past to disqualify themselves, we are not victims of our past and shouldn't use our past as a disqualifier. God told me my past was not actually the problem, but the conclusions I made about myself when the past happened were the problem. Empowered people have overcome victim mindsets and discovered that we may not be able to change our past, but we can create new conclusions.

One of the things I've discovered is that we first have to bring dominion (control) over our own thoughts and attitudes before we can release authority and have influence on the atmosphere around us (inner victory precedes outer victory). Bill Johnson, Senior Leader of Bethel Church in Redding, California, says, "People who only access the mercy of God will remain under the forces which push them to sin. They are forgiven, but still a slave." And that's where a lot of us are. We know how to access the mercy of God for forgiveness of our sins, **but too often we haven't yet learned how to access our new divine nature, so we do not yet believe that we have been empowered for righteousness and power, so we never become an influential person (Romans 6:16).** We are forgiven, but remain powerless.

Three key empowering beliefs to build within ourselves so we can move forward in becoming empowered and being empowering are: The "I have more than enough" belief, the "I am more than enough" belief, and the "I have dominion" belief.

THE "I HAVE MORE THAN ENOUGH" BELIEF

Many of us believe and see physical proof of the fact that lack is an ongoing problem and struggle in our lives. Our brains are always looking for proof of what they already believe. You won't see yourself clearly until you believe what God says about you. Therefore the greater truth is that we have more than enough. "As His divine power has given to us all things that pertain to life and godliness, **through the knowledge of Him** who called us by glory and virtue" (2 Peter 1:3). Notice that we can't access what has been given to us except through knowledge or a transformed mind.

We so commonly experience running out of time, energy, and money, but the truth is that by His divine power, He has given us everything we need for life and godliness, **and this comes through the knowledge we have of Him.** We tend to think "if He wants me to have it, He will zap me with it," meanwhile He is waiting for us to renew our minds with the truth that we have been already given everything we need to be empowered in both life and godliness. In other words, we have everything we need to succeed in this realm and the supernatural realm.

For instance, the children of Israel were led out of Egypt but they didn't believe they had the ability to defeat the giants in the Promised Land. **They were in a sense saved, but they were enslaved to their own beliefs that they were made smaller than the enemy.** They believed they had to wait on God to overcome the enemy. I can imagine the Israelites walking through the desert, saying, "God has given us manna. He has made our clothes not wear out. Clearly when He wants us to enter the Promised Land. He will remove the giants because we are just lowly slaves with no power or ability to conquer them." That was not the truth for them or for us. If we want to leave the wilderness, we cannot wait for God to zap us into the Promised Land. "And from the days of John the Baptist until now the Kingdom of heaven suffers violence, and the violent take it by force" (Matthew 11:12). God created us to be powerful, and we have access to His Kingdom and promises, but the beliefs that disqualify us from defeating our giants will keep us from inheriting our promised land.

Often we allow the constraint of time to disempower us. We think we are limited to the natural realm of time. Time often makes us feel like slaves. We allow ourselves to become victims to time. The power we give to time often produces stress or fear. When under stress and fear, our brains do not function at full capacity, which causes us to need even more time to accomplish our tasks. The negative emotions caused by a sense of lack actually work against us because they create what I call static in our brain and atmosphere. Our brain is so busy trying to cope with the negative emotion that it cannot flow in its full creativity. This also creates static in our spiritual atmosphere that hinders our ability to hear what God is saying about the situation. You have probably had times when you were afraid or stressed and could not hear God. The problem is not that God is silent during those times, but rather your reception is being affected because of your emotions. I have learned to not even try to hear God about a problem until I have recovered my peace through dwelling on His goodness and power. When our belief system becomes "I have more than enough," we become empowered. As we begin to declare things like the following, we will increasingly see it in our experience: "I have more than enough time. I wanted two hours to get that job done, but I only have one. Somehow God will help me to do it because I'm not just flesh, but I am supernatural, and He can cause me to get this done in less time." Declarations like this will strengthen us and help us to be at peace even when it seems we don't have enough because we know that He has given us all things, and He has more than enough.

THE "I AM MORE THAN ENOUGH" BELIEF

Inadequacy is a common disempowering belief. Many of us spend more time defending and renewing our minds with the belief that we are "not enough," rather than creating a belief based on the truth that God never asks us to do something that is not in our nature or ability to accomplish. Because we cannot consistently do what we don't believe we are, we would be wise to focus more on our identity than on our actions. For instance, when God told Moses to go talk to Pharaoh, Moses' first response was to list his inadequacies. He told God that he stuttered and could not speak well, and he did not have a position that enabled him to have influence with Pharaoh. He believed he wasn't enough and that Pharaoh wouldn't listen to him. "But Moses said before the Lord, 'Behold, I am of uncircumcised lips, and how shall Pharaoh heed me?' (Exodus 6:30). Then the Lord said to Moses, 'See I have made you as God to Pharaoh'" (Exodus 7:1). Instead of doubting himself, Moses needed to see himself as God had made him.

One sign that we struggle believing we are more than enough is that we look for confirmation of lack. In other words, we will look for proof that we are not enough. When Steve and I first got married, I had really low self-esteem and always felt inadequate. I didn't realize it back then, but I was always looking for proof that I was inadequate.

I used to like waiting until the morning to do the dinner dishes from the previous evening so I could do them all at once. But often Steve would get up before me and do the dishes himself. By doing this, I thought he was saying that I was a bad wife; if I was a good wife, I'd have the dishes done right away. Years later, when I heard about the five love languages, I realized that one of Steve's main love languages is acts of service. Because I was subconsciously looking for proof that I wasn't enough, I interpreted his actions as "You're not enough," when he was actually trying to say, "Wendy, I love you."

Some other indicators that I was defending negative beliefs about myself (often subconsciously) were:
- Looking for proof that people didn't value me
- Assuming something was wrong with me when promises were delayed; I believed my flaws disqualified me from the promises, which meant I could never stand in faith for them
- Not counseling others because I believed I was not enough
- Sabotaging my life by living from fear and unworthiness

Many empower others more than themselves because they believe in others more than they believe in themselves. Sometimes we may even think we believe in ourselves, but we have an underlying, subconscious belief that disagrees with our conscious thinking. If we don't have a deep revelation of our identity in Christ, or we think our nature somehow disqualifies us from what God has called us to do, then this will manifest in how we talk to ourselves and what we believe we are capable of. We will not aggressively go after our inheritance with a weak hope that we have what it takes. Timidity does not kill giants. If you do not believe you are more than enough, you will quit at the first sign of "proof" that it is true.

THE "I HAVE DOMINION" BELIEF

The level of dominion or authority we believe we carry will determine the level of empowerment we experience. If we believe our lives our out of our control even at a low level, it will totally disempower us. Romans 8:11 tells us the good news that the same Spirit that raised Christ from the dead dwells in us. That means that we have resurrection power not only flowing in us but out of us. Another scripture that helps us understand this is Ephesians 1:18-23: "I pray that the eyes of your heart may be enlightened in order that you may know the hope to which He has called you, the riches of His glorious inheritance in His holy people, and His incomparably great power for us who believe. That power is the same as the mighty strength He exerted when He raised Christ from the dead and seated Him at His right hand in the heavenly realms, far above all rule and authority, power and dominion, and every name that is invoked, not only in the present age but also in the one to come. And God placed all things under His feet and appointed Him to be head over everything for the church, which is His body, the fullness of Him who fills everything in every way." Pay special attention to the fact that God wants us to understand the riches of our inheritance and the incomparable power that works in us who believe. Remember also that the first job given to man through Adam in Genesis 1:26 was to take dominion over the earth and all the creatures. We tend to think our dominion was revoked because of the fall of man in Genesis 3, rather than focusing on the truth that Jesus reinstated our authority and power with His resurrection. One of our main battles in life is to believe this.

What is the evidence that we do not believe in the dominion given to us? The first clue is a feeling that we have no control over our lives. When life feels out of control, there's this sense of helplessness. We can feel like everyone else is in charge of our lives and even our emotions. We feel like we can't do anything to stop this train wreck or have any power over its effect on our lives.

Another clue that we don't have a full understanding of our dominion is that we spend a lot of emotional energy meditating on how we can keep what we have safe. Have you ever done that? Do you know why we try to keep what we have safe? It's because, deep down, we think we received what we have by luck and there's no way we're going to get it again if we lose it. If you have a good position and you're worried about losing it, it may be because you don't believe you earned that position because of who you are – you think you got it by luck. You can be at a certain standard of living and yet be afraid of losing it because you don't believe you have it because of who you are. The belief system to overcome this is: "I have dominion" (like we read in Ephesians 1:20). Remind yourself what you have is not because of luck, other people, or God sovereignly letting you have something you don't deserve. You have it because of who God has made you.

Romans 8:19 says, "For the earnest expectation of the creation eagerly waits for the revealing of the sons of God. For the creation was subjected to futility, not willingly, but because of Him who subjected it in hope; because the creation itself also will be delivered from the bondage of corruption into the glorious liberty of the children of God." At the fall, not only did we come under the corrupting effects of sin and sickness, but creation itself also came under that same corruption. It says God subjected the earth to that same thing in the hopes that we, as His people, will begin to deliver the earth when we come into a revelation of who we are and what we carry. He gave us dominion over the plants and the animals. It's not going to be enough to just join an environmental group to save the planet. We'll have a much greater effect if we realize who we are and that we can speak to waters to become clean and restore land that has become defiled. The first environmentalist act was in Exodus 15:25 when Moses threw a stick in the bitter waters and made it fit to drink.

A personal example is when God started speaking with me about how I was eating. When God first started telling me to eat right, my mind started to fill up with arguments. My hopeless, non-dominion self was thinking, "How can I eat right when the very vegetables I buy don't have the same nutrients they used to have because of what they put into the ground? And then there are the pesticides and all the poisons they put on them. Some people say to buy organic, but I can't afford organic. So I am helpless and out of control, and I cannot eat right!" The first step in order to change is to believe there is always a solution, so I started declaring that my body is under a covenant of health and eating right is easy!

We can unintentionally embrace a hopelessness and non-dominion attitude in many areas of our lives. When we first started traveling extensively seven years ago, I put on a lot of weight. I wanted to lose weight, but I had a long list of arguments and reasons why I couldn't lose weight. I am back on track now with losing weight because I decided not to be a victim to any of those things. I have also found a way to consistently eat healthy food. We can never overcome what we believe we are victim to. Let's choose to believe that through Christ we can overcome all things!

As Christians we're not called to just endure hardship – we are called to be overcomers. This is part of what it means to be empowered. God has called us to overcome, not just endure. We have dominion. If we believe we have dominion, we will think differently. We can change things. We can pray over them. There's always a solution, especially if we believe we are supernatural. We have dominion over the earth and atmosphere. Even though I am not experiencing this to the fullest measure in my life (none of us are), I am on a journey to seeing it increase. I am truly learning how to empower myself.

Although I've identified three key beliefs for empowering ourselves, other beliefs exist that are unique to each individual that we need to address as well. Some steps to help you in the process of identifying beliefs that need to be upgraded are:

- **Identify disempowering beliefs.** If a belief doesn't give you hope, then it's not empowering you.
- **Pay attention to what you usually say.** As my husband says, "Become a student of your words." Your self-talk will reveal which beliefs need an upgrade and which beliefs are good.
- **Be aware of repeated cycles in your life.** What roadblocks seem to consistently repeat themselves? Often these are a big clue into your belief system.
- **Ask yourself, "What do I complain about that stops me from living a life of increasing abundance?"** What you think is stopping you probably isn't what's really stopping you. Most likely your belief about it is the problem.
- **Be aware that your quality of life is influenced by your self-worth.** If you want to live at a higher level in any area, take steps to improve the beliefs that create your sense of self-worth.

Once you've identified some beliefs that need to be upgraded, then you will be able to create new beliefs in these areas. This may be challenging as your old beliefs will likely feel very real, but be full of hope for your beliefs to change. Keep in mind that people who try something new often experience failure over and over, but be persistent and you will see new beliefs begin to manifest, and your life will come into alignment with your new beliefs.

One of the biggest beliefs that will disempower us is that we are just human bodies trying to live spiritually. Each of our spirits exists forever, and they have more substance and more power than we know. We became a new creation when we were born again, and we get to learn what it looks like to live with an awareness of our spirits, rather than living as mere humans. "Therefore, if anyone is in Christ, he is a new creation; old things have passed away; behold, all things have become new" (2 Corinthians 5:17). For more insight as to how to live from your spirit, please see my book *Living From the Unseen* in which I share my personal journey with this and give practical tools for how to live from the unseen realm (the Kingdom of Heaven).

As I close this chapter, I release revelation over each person reading this book. May God bless you on your journey of not only becoming an empowering person, but also on your journey of creating beliefs that will leave you empowered.

> When we say negative things about ourselves and believe that we don't have what it takes to succeed in life, we actually disempower ourselves in respect to our destiny. – Michael Brodeur

WHAT WE'RE NOT SAYING

- We are not saying that there aren't serious challenges that arise in life or that we are never to mourn. (We are saying we can have hope for the future because we will never settle for anything but what Christ paid for.)
- We are not saying that we could never have seasons in which we have financial or other areas of lack. (We are saying we are on a journey of experiencing a decreasing measure of lack in all areas of life.)
- We are not saying that walking in dominion means we as Christians want to control the lives of other people. (We are saying we are in control of our lives no matter what others do.)

DECLARATIONS

- I empower myself greatly by having a deep and growing revelation of my identity in Christ.
- I am a new creation full of eternal life.
- I am hopeful about myself.

BEING AN EMPOWERING PERSON

Empowerment is a way of life, not a management style.

Steve Backlund

mpowering people are empowering in every situation, not just when they're leading. They don't just empower when they are functioning as leaders, but it is something they do all the time. This lifestyle is an overflow of who they are. It is a way of life, not a management style.

This empowering lifestyle overflows from many qualities, but one of the most important is this: Truly empowering people actually like people. It won't work to say, "I love people, but I don't really like them." Nor will it be effective to pretend to like people.

My own journey into really liking people at a higher level is illustrated by two characters in the story of the Prodigal Son in Luke 15. The father loves and likes the prodigal son, while the elder brother may love his brother, but it is clear by his response that he really does not like him. The elder brother:
- Was critical and fault-finding
- Was more focused on behavior than heart connection
- Believed he understood the true motives of his brother
- Was prideful, condescending, and had an attitude of superiority
- Was aloof and separated himself from someone who he determined was a failure
- Had an "it's not fair" attitude

Although I was not an overt elder brother when I was a younger leader, I did carry too many of these qualities inwardly, which hindered how much people could be empowered by me. I focused on verses like Jeremiah "The heart of man is desperately wicked …" rather than the higher truth of "know no man after the flesh …" (Jeremiah 17:9; 2 Corinthians 5:16).

As I reflected more about this, I realized my lack of liking people at a deep level resulted from my belief that God did not like me at a deep level. We truly do love our neighbors as we love ourselves.

Elder brothers tend to first see what is wrong with a person or place, while the father's default is to first see what is right with a person or place. This tendency to first see the best is the nature of true mothers and fathers. For instance, if their son just committed murder, the parents would probably say, "I know he is a good boy. There are so many good things in him." This does not mean we overlook wrongs being done, but the heart default is seeing the best.

The father in Luke 15:
- Focused more on having a heart connection than addressing poor conduct
- Ran with excitement toward the son
- Believed in the son more than the son believed in himself

As we mature, we will become more like a father or mother to others through our attitude toward them. This has certainly happened for me. As I experienced God's love and belief in me during my own struggles, I found myself increasingly releasing this belief and love to others in my life. As I did, they started rising up and being more than they thought they could be. I did not know it then, but I was creating a culture of empowerment around me.

This foundation of loving, liking, and believing in people creates the framework for being an empowering leader. On this foundation, other great qualities are built.

YOU KNOW YOU ARE AN EMPOWERING PERSON IF:

You make people feel important and valuable – You have an unusual ability to make people feel important around you. This is done by actively listening, being fully present, and noticing, commenting on, and pulling on their strengths in your relationship.

You thank people specifically, and you are a radical encourager – You notice and affirm the good things others are doing. You genuinely believe the people in your life can do great things, and you believe these people could be one encouragement away from a tipping point in their lives.

You think "win-win" – You don't think "win-lose" with you benefiting from the relationship, but not them. Nor do you think "lose-win" by having a misguided, self-abasing servanthood attitude that causes personal and family problems for you while the other person benefits from your sacrifice. On the contrary, empowering people look for ways to have a mutual benefit in all relationships. This comes from a mindset that every person has something good to offer, and "everyone" includes us.

You really see people – You are not self-absorbed, but you express delight in meeting someone or seeing someone again (even if this delight is just for a brief moment).

You have a "work yourself out of a job" mentality – You instinctively pass on to others what you know. You embody the master and apprentice culture that has dominated most of mankind's history.

You understand the normal pattern of relationships – You realize many of life's closest and most meaningful relationships go through these three stages: 1) Excitement, 2) Disappointment, and 3) Growth.

You believe a people's negative qualities are usually immature aspects of strengths in their life – You know as you are able to celebrate a person's strength, then the likelihood of having an empowering relationship dramatically increases.

You include others in what you do – You look for ways to have others work with you, minister with you, sit in on important meetings with you, travel with you, etc.

You are not afraid of messes, nor do you overreact when they happen – You realize there will be some "messes" made by those being empowered (even if thorough training is done). Also, empowered leaders know that their response to these messes is an important factor in whether people will ultimately thrive under their leadership.

You give others an opportunity to influence you – You believe everyone has something significant to contribute (e.g., an idea, a unique perspective, a life story, etc.). This belief causes empowering people to value relationships at a higher level, and it increases the likelihood of people thriving around them.

You have a strategy in how to lessen emotional disappointment in relationships – You decrease relational "mind games" by proactively communicating how you see the nature of the relationship. You decrease the likelihood of future relational challenges by intentionally addressing the most likely reasons for future disappointment.

You hear key things people say – You take note and remember key things people say and mention these in future conversations and communication with them. By doing so, you send the message: "Your life and your input are important to me."

You regularly use your favor to help open doors for others – You realize stewarding your favor well means you will endorse the faithful ones in your life to key influencers you know.

You are intentional in the meetings you have with people – You maximize meetings by giving thought as to how the time together can be the most beneficial. You realize that five minutes of proactive thinking about these times will likely make the meeting five times more powerful. These numbers increase even more if this forethought is done days or weeks before the meeting.

You help people get some "wins" in their lives – You look for ways to help people gain momentum by helping them succeed in small ways.

You prioritize heart connections – You cause other people to feel connected to you through humility, empathy, listening, appreciation, and honor.

You honor the priorities people have apart from their relationship with you – You are interested in and value the person's overall well-being, not just the things he or she can do for you.

You have a culture of feedback – You receive feedback, and you make it the norm to share about the positives and the areas needing improvement regarding emotions, actions, and relationships.

Here is a comparison of attributes of empowering and non-empowering people:

EMPOWERING	NON-EMPOWERING
Builds people	Uses people
Celebrates people on team	Feels threatened by strengths of others
"Send" people mentality	"Keep" people mentality
Seeks buy-in for big decisions	Decides and informs
Proactive	Reactive
"Skills" training mentality	"Keeping job" training mentality
Gives proactive, helpful feedback	Gives reactive feedback
Pursues feedback on leadership	Resistant to having personal feedback
Proactive feedback plan to others	Waits until angry or frustrated to correct
People focused	Task focused
Building "big people" focused	Building "big organization" focused
Thinks win-win	Team member winning not prioritized
Earns respect	Demands respect
Leadership training focused	Get job done focused
Shares leadership often	Reluctant to share leadership
Steps back for others	Hogs spotlight
Rarely uses command mode	Frequently uses command mode
Apologizes easily	Apology is difficult
Pulls insight out of others	Monopolizes conversations
Trains well, then delegates	Regularly under-delegates
Gives authority with responsibility	Micromanages
Humble	Self-focused
Genuinely interested in others	Little or no time to really know people
Promotes some more than others	Tries to make everything fair
Direct about concerns with team	Uses indirect comments to make point
Honoring	Controlling and manipulative
Thankful	Entitled
Teachable	Non-accountable
Resists "receiving" gossip	Embraces hearsay comments easily

You do not receive negative hearsay information shared to you about other people – You understand if you lower your opinion about another person based on unverified, negative information shared by another (or based on another's offense), then you reduce your influence in that person's life, and you will develop a pattern of behavior very detrimental to empowerment.

You identify and proclaim the unique giftings and attributes to those in your life – Like the angel did for Gideon in Judges 6, you see and speak about what people cannot see in themselves.

You are consistent in how you treat and respect people – You have the same level of kind-heartedness to the rich people in life as you do for those who are less fortunate. You honor all people.

You realize your words release death or life into your environment – You refrain from speaking negative identity statements and condescending comments in relationships. You create a positive, life-filled atmosphere through the intentional speaking of hope, appreciation, and encouragement.

You live a life of integrity – You know that dishonesty, breaking commitments, and the covering up of faults creates a lack of trust for you, which ultimately destroys an empowering culture.

You "date" people in smaller things before releasing them into higher responsibility – You give people opportunities to participate in your world, but you are not impulsive in giving titles or proclaiming "this is the one" language. You understand that trust is foundational to healthy relationships, and trust for one another is proved by walking through the joys and challenges of life together.

You have a leadership training mentality, not a "fix people's problems" mentality – You have compassion and help for people in crisis, but you are primarily focused on equipping people to connect with their life purpose. As you do this, it will help create vision for those in crisis, which is a key to their breakthrough.

You purpose to address three primary needs people have – 1) the need to be loved, 2) the need to belong, and 3) the need to be significant.

You have a strong sense of loyalty to the people on your team – Even though at times personnel changes will need to be made, you resist the tendency to vacillate back and forth in beliefs about team members. As Dean Ras, one of my former interns, says about deciding to marry someone, "Once the ring is on that is the one." This approach will cause you to remember why you chose your team members, which in turn will strengthen your faith for the relationships and ultimately increase the likelihood of team success.

You care for the whole person, not just what the person can do for you –You are sensitive to such things as people's connection to God, the health of their family, their financial situation, their need for rest and time off, their dreams and desires, and their current life battles.

CELEBRATE PROGRESS, NOT PERFECTION, IN YOUR EMPOWERMENT JOURNEY

When we look at a list like this, recognizing many areas for growth in ourselves might discourage us. If you are experiencing that emotion, we would encourage you to celebrate every step of progress you make, rather than focusing on areas you believe you are not advancing in.

RESIST THE URGE TO LABEL LEADERS OVER YOU AS NON-EMPOWERING

We cannot fully grow into being an empowering person if we walk in a continual attitude of criticism or hurt toward leaders over us. If we are called to be in a place where the culture of empowerment is not being demonstrated, then we have a great opportunity of learning how to maintain high-level beliefs about our leaders while seeking to influence the environment in a positive way. Obviously, we are not saying we should stay in an abusive situation, but we do need to understand there will never be a perfect leader over us. I have found that my response to the faults of a leader over me is a key factor in determining how ready I am to lead.

WHAT WE ARE NOT SAYING

- We are not saying if someone perceives us as not empowering, it automatically means we are not empowering.
- We are not saying we should keep chronically poor performers on our team.
- We are not saying employee retention is a bad thing.
- We are not saying we should sacrifice the vision and goals of the organization for one person's emotional well-being.
- We are not saying if you have any non-empowering attributes that it is impossible for you to be empowering.

DECLARATIONS

- I not only love people but also like people. My default is to first see the best in people.
- People feel important and valued around me.
- I create a positive, empowering atmosphere through intentionally speaking hope, appreciation, and encouragement.

EMPOWERING LANGUAGE

The future is in the mouths of intentional speakers.
Steve Backlund

STEVE'S EXPERIENCE

Like many of you reading this book, I did not grow up with many empowering words spoken to me from the influential people in my life. My father was a good man, but a person of few words. He told me when I did something wrong, but he did not speak identity or life purpose to me. My friends seemed to focus more on my faults and physical defects than on my good points. My mother was nurturing and very supportive, yet she too was limited in speaking empowering words.

I was outwardly successful in elementary and high school. Even so, I did not know who I was or what my purpose in life was. Besides my mom, I could count on one hand the people who truly empowered me during those years with their words – Mr. Sanderson (my little league coach), Mr. Ziegler (my eighth grade teacher), Mr. Dewell (my junior high Sunday School teacher), and Mrs. Riffenburg (my 12th grade government teacher). I did not know it, but one of the main reasons I was battling with insecurity was because I was in environments that spoke disempowering words to me but did not speak empowering words over me.

As a matter of fact, I was so desperate to be in a culture of empowering words that just one brief conversation caused me to choose my major in college. As a senior in high school, Mrs. Riffenburg took special interest in me and told me I would be good in government and politics. Because of this, I majored in political science when I went to university.

WORDS ARE POWERFUL

"Death and life *are* in the power of the tongue …" (Proverbs 18:21).

We have all experienced the power of words in our lives. We remember when a person we respect gave us a strong compliment or criticized us. These words became life or death to our beliefs about ourselves and our future.

Here is a lie many of us were told: "Sticks and stones may break your bones, but words can never hurt you." Wrong words can hurt people incredibly, but right words can create a launching pad for our future. "Pleasant words *are like* a honeycomb, sweetness to the soul and health to the bones" (Proverbs 16:24).

"Even a fool is counted wise when he holds his peace; when he shuts his lips, he is considered perceptive" (Proverbs 17:28).

The words we speak either corrupt the culture we are a part of or release grace into it. "Let no corrupt word proceed out of your mouth, but what is good for necessary edification, that it may impart grace to the hearers" (Ephesians 4:29). As we consider this, it is noteworthy to realize that one of the best definitions of grace is "the empowerment to do God's will."

WORDS ACTUALLY REVEAL WHAT WE REALLY BELIEVE

"Out of the abundance of the heart the mouth speaks" (Matthew 12:34).

On our journey in becoming a more empowering person who speaks empowering words, we will find ourselves saying things we ultimately don't want to say. Our beliefs about others, our circumstances, and ourselves will be revealed in our words. It is the wise leader who becomes a student of his or her own words. As we find ourselves regularly saying things that are not empowering, then it is time to go back to the chapter on empowering beliefs to upgrade what we believe so we can upgrade what we speak. Also, it is important to realize that upgrading our language will help improve our beliefs (Romans 10:17).

VERBAL LANGUAGE IS OUR MAIN METHOD OF COMMUNICATION TO OTHERS

People developed languages to be able to communicate effectively with others. Languages are comprised of many words that have their own distinct meaning. The Oxford English Dictionary lists more than 250,000 distinct words, not including many technical, scientific, and slang terms. The most effective communicators learn how to use the right words in the right way so others hear what the communicator wants them to hear.

Empowering leaders are not reactive speakers, but they are proactive and intentional in what they say to the individuals and groups they influence. They understand that just as there is an *English* language, there is also an *Empowerment* language. Specific words empower, just as other specific words disempower.

Of course, we realize that simply using the right language will not guarantee we will be empowering. Spoken words are only one part of the communication process. Empowering speakers will have love, empathy, and authenticity as the foundations to their words. As we truly embrace empowering beliefs, our words will be filled with life to transform the people around us.

Even though we embrace the truth that communication is much more than words spoken, we cannot downplay the reality of the power of specific words. Below are two lists that compare disempowering and empowering language.

LANGUAGE THAT DISEMPOWERS

I say this when I speak on the power of words: "One of the best things some people can do is just stop talking." I say this in semi-jest to get a point across. I refer to the story in Luke 1 when Zechariah is muted for nine months during his wife Elizabeth's pregnancy with John the Baptist. God could not trust Zechariah to talk around what He was doing.

It is probably not practical for us to not speak at all, but here are some things to avoid in our speaking:

- **Accusatory words** – Phrases that are dominated by the word "You." "You always ..." or "You never ..."
- **Labeling words** – Past-based identity statements spoken over people. "She is a very disorganized person."
- **Limiting words** – "You could never do that" or "That is impossible" or "You are non-administrative."
- **Prejudice words** – "Young people today are lazy!"
- **Victim words** – "Because of what has happened to you in the past, you need the government to take care of you. There is no other answer."
- **Guilt language** – "If you were a good Christian or person, you would ..."
- **Bitterness language** – "You have hurt me so much. You are a horrible person."
- **Abusive authority language** – "God will be angry with you if you don't do what I say."
- **Negative identity words** – "You are stupid" or "You don't care" or "You are selfish."
- **Law words** – "The letter kills, but the Spirit gives life" (2 Corinthians 3:6). "The letter" is when preachers and teachers tell people what they are supposed to do much more than telling them what Christ has done and who they are in Him.
- **Words spoken from frustration** – "God's presence won't manifest because of the people in the back who are talking. Stop talking and start loving God!!!"
- **Manipulation words** – "Mom, I hate you" or "If you really loved me, you would ..." or "If you don't give to our ministry in the next 30 minutes, you will miss a radical blessing from God."
- **Controlling words** – "You don't want to see me mad, so you better do this" or "If you leave our church, you will be out of the will of God." Also, the overuse of the following phrases would tend to be controlling as well: "You must," "You need to," and "You should."
- **Assumption words** – "All of you know the story of Jonathan and David."
- **Condescending words** – "I am not sure if you have heard of the Apostle Paul, but he made a big difference in the Bible."

- **"You are not capable of understanding what you need" words** (often spoken by elites in church, government, and education) – "You are not capable of really understanding what is best."
- **Projection words** – Giving the impression that what we are experiencing is what everyone else is experiencing too. "You know when someone doesn't follow through and you feel disappointed and get upset …"
- **Hindering words** – People who don't think their words are powerful will more frequently say things like, "My back is killing me" or "That is driving me crazy."
- **Overusing "you" phrases instead of "we" phrases** – "You need to read the Bible" versus "We need to read the Bible."
- **"You are stupid" words** – "I can't believe you do not know how to do that."
- **Insecure or false humility words** – "I know I am not smart enough to really contribute to this conversation, but I have an idea."

The non-empowering leader will tend to use language to control others through creating a climate of fearing punishment, shame, and guilt. But the empowering leader will inspire others by releasing hope and confidence in the people he or she leads.

LANGUAGE THAT EMPOWERS

"Death and life are in the power of the tongue" (Proverbs 18:21). It is true that death is in the power of our words, **but the greater truth is that there is the power of life in our words.** Here is a list of words that will create great life around us:

- **Encouraging words** – "You are making a difference around here."
- **Positive identity words** – "You are a person of great strategic insight. This gifting is taking our organization to higher levels."
- **Specific thanksgiving words** – "Here are three reasons I appreciate you: 1) You make people feel valued in your presence, 2) Your belief in me has been a great strength to me, and 3) Your prayer and worship life inspires me."
- **"I understand you" words** – "I know it's important to you that I keep my room clean so here is my plan to do this more consistently."
- **"I see you" words** – "I notice how you always make new people feel welcome and included."

- **"I need you" words** – "I just wanted to let you know that we really need you here. You make us so much more successful."
- **"Win-win" language** – "You help me so much. What are the two most important things I can do to help you see your life dreams fulfilled?"
- **"I am proud of you" words** – "I was thinking today of how proud I am of you. You are reliable, you do things with excellence, and you represent us so well."
- **"You are significant and important" words** – "You are important. What you do is connected to a bigger purpose and plan. We would not be nearly as successful without you."
- **Prophetic destiny language** – "You are being prepared for bigger influence in the days ahead. This position you have now is training you for those things."
- **"You've got what it takes" words** – "You can do it! Nothing is impossible for you!"
- **Hope-filled words** – "There is always a solution. I don't know what it is, but God has one for this situation."
- **"Giving the benefit of the doubt" words** – "I missed the meeting because it wasn't on my calendar, but I might have missed something that was said about it happening in a conversation we had."
- **Celebration words** – "Hey everyone, I just wanted to let you know that Melissa has done a great job with the hope project."
- **"You have a unique and strategic assignment" words** – "Your temperament, your experience, and your skill set make you uniquely gifted for a special assignment. I would love to help you clarify the details of it."
- **Declarative faith statement words** – "Right now God is freeing people from depression" or "In this meeting people are getting physically healed."
- **"I feel" words** – "I feel like you frequently misunderstand me," or "I feel like your reaction to this circumstance indicates you might have a problem with what I have done."
- **True humility words** – "I have also struggled with that. Here is what the Lord showed me to help me to grow in victory in that area."

FIVE PHRASES TO RELEASE LIFE AND STRENGTHEN RELATIONSHIPS

1. **I am proud of you** – Many people never hear these words. When a pastor or leader says, "I am proud of you for _____," it helps meet a deep need in people's hearts.

2. **I am so glad you are on my team** – Don't take for granted whom God has given you.

3. **I need you** – These words are powerful. They are even stronger when we get specific. "I need your ability to release the supernatural in my life and in this ministry."

4. **I really admire you for _____** – "I really admire the way you love people" or "I really admire how faithful you are to worship." It is powerful when we get specific.

5. **I am committed to helping you reach your dreams** – Our ministry is to build people and release them into their God-given purposes. When we encourage people's dreams and come up with ideas and opportunities to make them happen, we will increase our heart connections with those we lead.

EMPOWERING SELF-TALK

One of the areas that can be easily overlooked with our language is our self-talk. How are we talking to ourselves? Are we disempowering or empowering ourselves with our words? My wife, Wendy, says that if we wouldn't counsel someone else with it, then we shouldn't counsel ourselves with it. For example, we wouldn't say to someone we're meeting with, "There is no hope for you. You will never be healed. You are fat and ugly. You are not smart enough. You can't change." These are extreme examples, and although we may not overtly talk like this to ourselves, how many of us have ever thought or said things such as, "I don't look good," "I can't do that," or "I don't make a difference" to ourselves? Part of being a student of our words is paying attention to what we are saying to ourselves, and then being committed to creating life and empowering ourselves through hope-filled self-talk based on our identity in Christ.

Here are a few other areas in which we have the opportunity to be empowering and to model that for others:

EMPOWERING AND NON-EMPOWERING LANGUAGE IN SERMONS/TEACHINGS

Non-Empowering

- Focuses almost exclusively on action and "You are not a good Christian unless you do ..." language
- Is rooted in the belief that the listeners do not really want to do the right thing
- Frequently uses phrases like "You must," "You should," or "You need to"
- Uses subtle or overt guilt to motivate: "Only 10% of you in this church tithe, and that is a travesty" or "If you are a real part of this church family, you will be at our special service tonight with Brother and Sister Onfire"
- Includes very little laughter

Empowering

- Focuses on telling people who they are much more than telling them what to do
- Is rooted in the belief that the listeners want to do the right thing
- Includes joy and laughter
- Focuses on creating a climate of hope the listeners can tangibly feel

ANNOUNCEMENTS/EVENT INVITATIONS

"Come to the volunteer opportunity meeting this Wednesday evening! An important part of being in our church family is to serve us and our church body, and it's biblical to serve. Come find out which areas we need help in, and be sure to sign up for all the ones you can help with. We will see you there!!!"

- What is a more empowering way to announce this meeting?
- How much would you be inspired to serve in this environment?

One area where we can see the difference between empowering and non-empowering language is in our church announcements or invitations to events. In empowering invitations, we assume the people want to do the right thing and that our event is not the only thing they have to do. So instead of saying "See you there," we would say something like "If you are able to attend this event, we believe it will be life-changing."

Here is an upgraded announcement for the same event:

"This Wednesday evening, you will have an opportunity to meet with our team leaders to hear their hearts about the ministries they oversee. You will learn more about how these ministries are powerfully impacting lives and how you can volunteer on one of the teams. This is a great way to connect with other like-hearted people. If you are looking for a way to invest your time and gifts into our church, then this meeting is for you.

EMAILS

Dear Fred,

I noticed you were late again today. It seems our conversations about this issue in your life are not working. It is obvious you do not value what I say. You have been playing this game of seeing what you can get away with for too long. I am going to report this to Mr. Smith, and he will not be happy. For the sake of your job, never be late again.

Very truly,
Abner

- What is wrong with the above email?
- What can you conclude about the level of empowerment in this environment?
- What are some keys to writing an email that addresses an issue with an employee/team member?

Here is an example of a more empowering email for the same situation:

Dear Fred,

I trust you are having a great day.

I noticed you were late again today. I am somewhat perplexed because you had indicated to me in our recent conversation your commitment to punctuality. I believe you are sincere in this, but it appears you still need a greater plan to make this happen. Please let me know if I'm missing anything in how I'm seeing this. I will be speaking with Mr. Smith about this. We would love to strategize with you about how to remedy this.

You and I both know this tendency will need to be remedied for you to continue your employment here. Mr. Smith and I both desire for you to continue here to keep growing in your job skills and, more importantly, your life.

I look forward to hearing from you this week about your plan to address your tardiness so Mr. Smith and I will have the needed confidence and trust in you as one of our advancing team members.

We thank you for the many ways you have been a strength to our company.

Yours truly,
Abner

- It's important to remember to prioritize relationship and to let that guide the writing of our emails. There will be times when short emails will suffice, but for potentially sensitive issues, be sure to include an opening and conclusion that make it clear you care about the person.
- Please note this email makes it clear they had already discussed this in person. It's wise to have face-to-face conversations when addressing any delicate or new issues.

PHONE CALLS

Harry Ina Hurry calls his assistant and says, "Hello, Sophie. I needed the sales report for last quarter on my desk five minutes ago. Stop whatever you're doing and bring it to me right now." He hangs up without waiting for a response from Sophie.

- How do you think this call would make Sophie feel?
- What is it assuming about Sophie and her current circumstances?

Here is how this phone call could look if Harry wasn't in such a hurry and genuinely cared for his employees:

Harry says, "Hello Sophie. I have a board meeting in twenty minutes and I need to bring the sales report for last quarter with me. You're usually so on top of things that I just now realized I don't have it here yet. Is everything okay?

Sophie replies, "Thanks for asking. The school nurse called and my son injured his arm. I'm already on my way from the printer and will be there with the report in one minute. Olivia is going to help you with anything you need while I go take care of my son."

Harry smiles and says, "You are so proactive. I appreciate how you've already asked someone to fill in for you before I even knew there was a problem. See you in a minute."

- We're not saying that we don't ever ask for things, but the way we ask for them makes a big difference.
- It's important that we give people the benefit of the doubt and don't make assumptions. Remember that we tend to judge ourselves by our intentions and others by their behavior. Let's be empowering not only in our words, but also in our thoughts toward others.
- When we do treat people without honor, admitting our mistake and apologizing is so important to maintaining heart connections and a culture of empowerment.

THE FUTURE IS IN THE MOUTHS OF INTENTIONAL SPEAKERS

It is not the absence of negative speech that creates a truly empowering culture, but it is the presence of life being spoken. Life truly is in the power of the tongue. "By the blessings of the upright, the city is exalted; but by the mouth of the wicked it is torn down" (Proverbs 11:11).

Old Testament leaders like Isaac and Jacob understood the power of intentionally speaking blessing over individuals, which affected future generations (Hebrews 11:20). This was part of their strategy to empower people with a divine force that propelled them to a place of influence and blessing. They believed their words were powerful and would shape history. Empowering leaders today will believe the same thing and will strategically speak to unlock the destinies of the people in their lives.

THE ROLE OF LAUGHTER IN RELEASING EMPOWERING LANGUAGE

As we have seen in this chapter, empowering leaders choose their words carefully in public messages and in private conversations. But we all know the right words with the wrong attitude will not empower those around us. I have found laughter can be a great help in causing the spirit attached to our words to be healthy.

In my teachings on joy and laughter, I frequently share two phrases that are important to this topic of empowering language. The first is "Laughter cleans out the pipes," and the second is "To laugh, you have to let go of something."

Have you ever drank good water out of bad pipes? It could be wonderful water, but because the pipe is tainted with rust or something else, it is difficult to swallow. That is the experience people have at times with the truth we speak. They might know it is truth, but it is difficult for them to swallow because the "pipe" it went through was tainted with frustration, bitterness, criticism, victimhood, discouragement, or something else.

We can take our empowerment to a higher level by valuing laughter. Hilarity is one of the best ways to clean out our pipes so the words we speak don't have negative spiritual substances attached to them.

We let go of things when we laugh. For instance, we cannot hold onto frustration and still really laugh. We will first need to be willing to let go of frustration in order to laugh. We also cannot hold onto disappointment and laugh. As we "let go" of these hindrances of our influence, we will find our empowerment increasing.

Here is a final phrase I share when I travel and speak: "I have a difficult time trusting the perspective of any Christian leader who does not laugh a lot." I realize we are not supposed to laugh all the time, but the laughter-impaired person will often have a "pipe issue" that hinders the receptivity others have toward him or her.

WHAT WE ARE NOT SAYING

- We are not saying we will never have seasons in relationships where our focus is more on a person's conduct than on positive encouragement to him or her.
- We are not saying we won't at times have to have firm boundaries with certain individuals, which will greatly limit how much they are empowered by us.
- We are not saying we won't ever need to rebuke people.
- We are not saying if someone interprets our language as disempowering, it automatically means our language is disempowering.

DECLARATIONS

- The words I speak continually create an atmosphere of life, healthy relationships, hope, and personal vision for everyone present.
- My words contain grace, empowering people toward godly living and into incredible influence.
- I use my words intentionally to empower people and to advance them into their destiny.

ESTABLISHING A CULTURE OF EMPOWERMENT

Being an empowering leader is not something you do,
but it is more importantly something you are.

Steve Backlund

I n my book *Victorious Mindsets*, I share 50 mindsets for victorious living. The truths of this hope-filled devotional focus on Romans 12:2 – "be transformed by the renewing of your mind." The renewing of the mind is not something that happens by osmosis, but it occurs by believing specific truths. As we believe the truth in a particular area of life, we are made free in that aspect of our living (John 8:32).

Two of the ideas I share in *Victorious Mindsets* are applicable in this chapter. They are:

- **"I Realize There Are Few 'Normal' Weeks"** – I remember as a young leader I would say practically every week, "This is not a normal week. I cannot do what I planned to do." I found that I was hindered from my goals and priorities because unexpected things happened (or I did not feel as energetic as I thought I would). Finally, I realized I would need to learn to thrive in non-normal weeks, or else I would not accomplish much at all in my life.
- **"I Put Things in My Path to Bump Into"** – I like to play golf, but I recognized if I did not get a good plan, I would regularly misplace or lose my pitching wedge. Here is what happened far too often: I would hit the ball close to the green, move my golf cart near the green, and then take

my pitching wedge and putter from the cart and walk to where the ball was. I would use the pitching wedge to hit the ball to the green and put the pitching wedge down on the ground at that spot. I would then walk to where I had hit the ball on the green and putt the ball in the hole. As I would walk back to the cart, I would forget to pick up my pitching wedge. I knew I needed a strategy to overcome this flaw. So I decided to place the pitching wedge between the hole and my cart so I would "bump" into to it as I made my way back to the cart. This has made a great difference in not losing this golf club. It more importantly taught me that finding ways to bump into things I deem important, but tend to forget, is an intentional step toward empowering leadership and a great tool for growth.

These two mindsets will be extremely helpful for the leader who wants to create an empowering culture in the organization he or she leads. First, we need to understand it will never be convenient to structure our lives and leadership to empower others. There will always be a reason why this is not a good time to do so. Secondly, we would be wise to proactively use our calendars so we will "bump into" important actions or meetings we might have a tendency to forget, but that are vital to a culture of empowerment.

As we consider this further, let's consider the four quadrants of time management:
- The urgent and important
- The important but not urgent
- The urgent but not important
- The not urgent and not important

Those who succeed learn how to do the important but not urgent things of life. Whether it is to change the oil in the car, spend time with God, spend quality time with our family, or exercise, these things are not screaming at us to be done, but doing them largely determines the quality of our lives.

One of the characteristics of an effective leader is they learn to do important things even when they don't feel like it. A main difference between successful and unsuccessful people is that successful people find ways to consistently do what they don't feel like doing, while unsuccessful people do not find those ways.

When we purpose to create a culture of empowerment in our organization, it puts a good pressure on us to upgrade our priorities to do the important, non-urgent things we often will not feel like doing. When we decide to care more about making others great more than we care about making ourselves great, we will indeed receive divine grace to become what Jesus called the "greatest." "But he who is greatest among you shall be your servant. And whoever exalts himself will be humbled, and he who humbles himself will be exalted" (Matthew 23:11-12).

He further debunks wrong leadership mindsets in this exchange with His disciples: "Now there was also a dispute among them, as to which of them should be considered the greatest. And He said to them, 'The kings of the Gentiles exercise lordship over them, and those who exercise authority over them are called "benefactors." But not so among you; on the contrary, he who is greatest among you, let him be as the younger, and he who governs as he who serves. For who is greater, he who sits at the table, or he who serves? Is it not he who sits at the table? Yet I am among you as the One who serves'" (Luke 22:24-27). This servant leadership style is not a wimpy, non-decisive, people-pleasing approach (Jesus was certainly not this), but it is a commitment to serving the longings and legitimate needs of people, including those on your team. This is the true foundation of empowerment, which focuses more on building people than building a ministry, business, or other organization.

In this chapter we will share with you 25 keys to establishing a culture of empowerment in your organization. Before we do, let's take a few more minutes to discuss even more *why* this is the best approach in leading others. If we don't fully understand the *why* in what we are doing, it will be difficult to consistently implement the 25 keys we are going to give you.

MORE REASONS TO LEAD IN AN EMPOWERING WAY

Besides servant leadership being the "greatest" path in leadership, here are four more reasons *why* it is a brilliant idea to lead in an empowering way:

- **It is a practical demonstration of 1 Corinthians 13 love** – "Love suffers long *and* is kind; love does not envy; love does not parade itself, is not puffed up; does not behave rudely, does not seek its own, is not provoked, thinks no evil; does not rejoice in iniquity, but rejoices in the truth; bears all things, believes all things, hopes all things, endures all things" (1 Corinthians 13:4-7). In the preceding verses of this chapter, we are told we can accomplish spectacular things, but if we don't live out this kind of love, it profits us nothing. Wow! Truly empowering leaders will treat all people with dignity and respect because they know people really matter.

- **We are to treat others as we would want to be treated** – "Whatever you want men to do to you, do also to them, for this is the Law and the Prophets" (Matthew 7:12). We are to treat others as we would want to be treated. How do we want leaders over us to treat us? The answer to this question will help develop our own leadership style. We receive further insight on this when a lawyer asked Jesus what the greatest commandment was. "Jesus said to him, 'You shall love the LORD your God with all your heart, with all your soul, and with all your mind. This is *the* first and great commandment. And *the* second *is* like it: You shall love your neighbor as yourself. On these two commandments hang all the Law and the Prophets'" (Matthew 22:37-40). The second greatest commandment is to love our neighbor as ourselves.

- **It is to be the focus of the most influential leaders in the church** – "And He Himself gave some *to be* apostles, some prophets, some evangelists, and some pastors and teachers, for the equipping of the saints for the work of ministry, for the edifying of the body of Christ" (Ephesians 4:11-12). Leaders are not to primarily do the "work of ministry," but they are to mainly focus on training and empowering others to do this. The Greek word for equip (*katartismon*) can be translated as to mend or to prepare. This implies a leadership emphasis of pouring into people.

- **It is the antidote to burnout, and a vital ingredient to longevity** – Moses was a great leader, but even he had to upgrade his leadership style into empowering others, rather than doing everything himself. Like so many of us, his motives were good, but he was not walking in wisdom. It took counsel from his father-in-law to bring dramatic change in how he led. "And so it was, on the next day, that Moses sat to judge the people; and the people stood before Moses from morning until evening. So when Moses' father-in-law saw all that he did for the people, he said, 'What *is* this thing that you are doing for the people? Why do you alone sit, and all the people stand before you from morning until evening?' And Moses said to his father-in-law, 'Because the people come to me to inquire of God. When they have a difficulty, they come to me, and I judge between one and another; and I make known the statutes of God and His laws.' So Moses' father-in-law said to him, **'The thing that you do *is* not good. Both you and these people who *are* with you will surely wear yourselves out. For this thing *is* too much for you; you are not able to perform it by yourself.** Listen now to my voice; I will give you counsel, and God will be with you: Stand before God for the people, so that you may bring the difficulties to God. And you shall teach them the statutes and the laws, and show them the way in which they must walk and the work they must do. Moreover you shall select from all the people able men, such as fear God, men of truth, hating covetousness; and place *such* over them *to be* rulers of thousands, rulers of hundreds, rulers of fifties, and rulers of tens. And let them judge the people at all times. Then it will be *that* every great matter they shall bring to you, but every small matter they themselves shall judge. So it will be easier for you, for they will bear the *burden* with you. **If you do this thing, and God so commands you, then you will be able to endure, and all this people will also go to their place in peace.'** So Moses heeded the voice of his father-in-law and did all that he had said. And Moses chose able men out of all Israel, and made them heads over the people: rulers of thousands, rulers of hundreds, rulers of fifties, and rulers of tens. So they judged the people at all times; the hard cases they brought to Moses, but they judged every small case themselves" (Exodus 18:13-23).

TWENTY-FIVE KEYS FOR ORGANIZATIONAL EMPOWERMENT

Here are 25 keys to establish a culture of empowerment in your organization. Some are specific actions to put on your calendar to "bump into" so the empowerment culture truly moves forward. Others are mindsets to shape your attitudes and priorities – which ultimately will shape your decisions.

1. **Have an incredible vision for your life and for the organization** – There is a difference between leaders and managers. Great leaders have a high purpose that others want to be a part of. They inspire people to do what they never thought they could do. Managers tend to be focused on things being done efficiently. Many of the 25 keys in this chapter emphasize having empowering management attributes, but empowering leaders cannot simply be good managers. "Big people" are not attracted to a small vision. If your vision is to pay the electric bill each month, only small-minded people will rally around that. If however your vision is to change the world (and you have some significant "wins" that people can see), then people with amazing talent and resources will be drawn to you.

2. **Live from a "call," not from good circumstances** – Double-mindedness is the enemy of great influencers, but having confidence we are "called by God" to lead in a specific place will create greater assurance in people to follow us. This confidence is not an arrogant "I am His chosen so you better follow or else," but it is a "knowing in your knower" that will be a strength against discouragement and negative circumstances.

3. **Keep believing in people when you don't want to** – Reaffirm that one of the greatest things you can do is to radically believe in the people you lead. Re-read the chapter on empowering beliefs so you will think about people the way God thinks about them. Also, realize those you are leading now are your training ground for greater influence in the days ahead.

4. **Take the necessary time to build trust for yourself in the eyes of others** – Don't take it personally if people are cautious in trusting you. Many are hesitant about leadership because of negative past experience. To build trust, stay away from these behaviors that would cause others to conclude you are not trustworthy:
   - Lack of integrity
   - Not admitting mistakes
   - Emotionally manipulating through anger, self-pity, or fear of punishment
   - Over-reacting when team members make a mistake
   - Micromanagement of the team
   - Making decisions without consulting key people affected by decisions

5. **Ask great questions** – Determine to understand people before you seek to be understood by them. Here are some sample questions to ask individuals, and at times, groups:
   - What kind of leadership style do you thrive the most under?
   - What things have past leaders (or bosses) done that have frustrated you and made it difficult to work under them? What positive traits of past leaders are you hoping to see here?
   - What ways have you most been a strength to your past leaders?
   - What tendencies have you had which caused difficulty for your past leaders?
   - Are you okay with me giving you feedback on how you are doing in your role here (on things you are doing well and areas you need to improve on)? When I have a concern with you, or see an area you can improve in, how can I best communicate this so you feel valued and empowered?

6. **Get a plan to overcome disappointment** – Remember that a common pattern in relationships is: 1) Excitement, 2) Disappointment, and 3) Growth or discontinuing the relationship. Yes, some relationships need to end, but more times than not, the disappointment is not terminal but an opportunity for growth in the relationship. The wise leader has a plan for how to emotionally handle being disappointed by those he or she is leading and has a plan to prepare others when he or she disappoints them.

7. **Prioritize heart connection and healthy relationships** – Empowering leaders create events and meetings where relationships can be established and deepened. These are not just token get-togethers to appease the socially-wired team members, but they are strategic personal and group meetings designed to increase the connectivity of the organization.

8. **Develop a leadership training program** – Here are some great questions for the leader to ask which will help guide the equipping of the team:
   - Is there adequate training before empowering others in leadership responsibilities?
   - How can I work myself out of my job by sharing my insights and experience?
   - What training should everyone receive?
   - What training should my core team receive?
   - What training should individuals receive that is unique to their job or assignment?
   - What creative ways can we offer our training?

> Empowering delegation must have a benefit for the person you're delegating to (e.g., a skill they can learn, a way for them to grow, etc.). Empowerment values team members by trusting (in every situation possible) their abilities and wisdom by including them in decision-making processes and giving them authority to make some decisions on their own. True empowerment can only occur when there has been adequate training and trust has been developed on the team.

9. **Continually think 'win-win" in relationships** – The empowering leader clarifies how each person causes the organization to win, and then also has discussions (group and private) on how you and your leadership can specifically create a win for the individual by being on your team.

10. **Develop an empowered structure of leadership** – It is important to clarify the organization's flow chart so it is clear who is responsible for various aspects and the people in its operation. The empowering leader will seek to work through the leader of a department regarding any concerns he or she has with people in that department, rather than bypassing the immediate supervisor in addressing a matter. The senior leader will prioritize his or her relationship with these "department heads" to ensure an ongoing heart connection is happening and quality exists in the department.

11. **Emphasize and train on healthy attitudes and communication in relationships** – Because many of the frustrations in organizations are relational, the empowering leader spends much time on training and having discussions regarding healthy team relationships. The leader also realizes they need to be proactive in discussions with core team members about how to do relationships in a healthy way with each other.

12. **Find ways to create buy-in for needed changes in the organization** – Empowering cultures are not democracies with everyone having an equal vote or equal influence, but they intentionally involve people in the process of decision making (especially those who will be impacted by the decision or those who have experience or expertise in what is being decided upon). This input can be received by:
    - Having regular brainstorming sessions on how to bring improvement
    - "Floating" ideas in team meetings concerning changes being considered for the future – this will lessen the likelihood of leaders "springing" decisions on their team that shocks and surprises them
    - Meeting personally with leaders and influencers to gauge "buy-in" before sharing potentially controversial changes in a team meeting
    - Meeting with leaders and others who will be most impacted by a future direction to see if there is anything being missed in the decision

13. **Reward innovative thinking that helps the organization go to the next level** – We will increase the likelihood of team members bringing transformational ideas if we reward innovative thinkers through recognition,

benefits, and/or a percentage of any financial increase resulting from the improvement.

14. **Clarify job descriptions** – It can be very frustrating if team members don't have clarity on what is expected of them or in what areas they will be evaluated on in job performance reviews.

15. **Have healthy, regular feedback and performance reviews** – Proactive leaders establish feedback and reviews to maintain productivity and positive relationships, while reactive leaders too often wait for a buildup of negative emotions before they address a problem on the team. This book has a sample job performance appraisal in the appendix. (Note: You as the main leader would be prudent to lead the way in having your own performance reviewed.)

16. **Establish the habit of team members setting goals** – An empowered culture is not simply a happy place where people like to work, but it actually is catalytic for greater things to be done. As part of the organization's goal setting plan, we suggest team members send a weekly email to their supervisor with the following in it:
    - The coming week's goals
    - Last week's goals with comments on it such as done, not done, etc.
    - Last week's high point (this can be job related or personal)
    - Last week's low point (job related or personal)

    We have sample weekly emails and more information on this in the appendix. Please note as you establish a goal setting culture that some of your most creative or most relational people may struggle with the rigidity and greater structure they perceive through the goal setting. We suggest you ask God for wisdom in how to keep them operating in their strengths while you help them become more efficient in leading their lives and their area of leadership. Finally, we also suggest you try the weekly goal setting plan on a smaller core team before implementing it throughout the organization.

17. **Create a culture of personal growth** – John Maxwell tells a story of someone who said they reached all of their life goals and then felt empty because there were no more goals to be reached. John said his problem was that he was goal focused, rather than growth focused. When we as leaders model a hunger for personal growth, and include our main leaders in this process, we will build big people around us. Some ideas in doing this are:

- Read the same book together and have a different person share a quote from it at group meetings.
- Attend a conference together.
- Offer training for life skills and for job related duties.

18. **Determine frequency of meetings with groups and individuals** – If we don't proactively put important meetings in our calendar, then our schedule will fill up with urgent but not important items. (We discuss this further in Chapter Ten.) As you consider your schedule, ask these questions:
    - What groups do I need to meet with and how often?
    - What individuals do I need to meet with and how often?
    - How long should these meetings be?
    - Who can help me cause these meetings to be empowering for those who come and for our organization?

19. **Care for the whole person, not just what they can do for you** – Most leaders do care for the well-being of their employees or team members, but sometimes get too busy to actually express that care on a regular basis. Most organizations are not going to provide pastoral care or counseling for their employees and volunteers, but much can be done to increase the team's sense they are really valued and cared for, and not just slaves of their overseers. Here are some ideas:
    - Designate one person on the team to oversee the encouragement and support of the others. They can be an "ear to the ground" so you will be aware at the earliest point of challenging or exciting things in your team members' lives. They can also help in remembering birthdays, anniversaries, and other important dates.
    - In the weekly goals email, have the team fill out their high and low for the past week. (And these highs and lows are not necessarily about their job.) This will keep their immediate supervisor current in what is happening in their lives. When appropriate, these highs and lows can be shared with other organizational leaders so the team can rejoice with them or stand with the individual in times of difficulty. (One note on these weekly reports: It is important that the immediate supervisor responds to the email with an email of his or her own acknowledging what was shared. It does not need to be a long email, but some response is necessary.)

20. **Encouragement and specific thanksgiving** – Empowering leaders are encouraging and thankful people. They find creative ways to keep

encouragement and gratitude at a high level. One way to do this is to enlist a volunteer or designate a staff person to help with this.

21. **Celebrate risk taking and innovation** – Winston Churchill said, "Success is moving from failure to failure without losing enthusiasm." Those who succeed most seem to also fail most. I used to think I had a successful year because I didn't fail much, but I realized that I never did anything either! Certainly we need to find ways to protect ourselves from failures that would be terminal for our organization, but remember this: *The same culture that created a Judas also created eleven world changers. If our goal is to prevent a Judas, we will never have world changers.* It is wise to develop and discuss your philosophy on taking risks and how it functions alongside wisdom and high buy-in. Great organizations have "dreamers," not just workers with a slave mentality.

22. **Embrace healthy conflict and disagreement** – If our team is afraid of sharing disagreements or concerns about proposed changes or our leadership style, then we need to take steps to increase our connection with individuals and we need to create more space in meetings for ideas and directional changes to be freely discussed.

23. **Share the glory for successes and be willing to take the blame for things that don't succeed** – Mark Twain said, "Great things can happen when you don't care who gets the credit." Empowering leaders are happiest when their team shines and has great success. Insecure, non-empowering leaders are threatened by the successes of others. Also, excellent leaders purpose to shoulder the blame for mistakes made by those working under them.

24. **Determine to walk in honor** – "'Honor your father and mother,' which is the first commandment with promise: 'that it may be well with you and you may live long on the earth'" (Ephesians 6:2-3). The promise concerning honoring your parents is mind-boggling. Honor is a life-producing attitude that is to be demonstrated in all relationships, not just concerning children and their parents. Empowering leaders understand every person is made in God's image and is worthy of honor. This is true regardless of race, gender, economic condition, age, or intelligence. As honor is released, personal and corporate empowerment follows.

25. **Be empowered by God** – God's assignments for our lives are impossible without His empowerment. "So he answered and said to me: 'This *is* the

word of the LORD to Zerubbabel: "Not by might nor by power, but by My Spirit," says the LORD of hosts. "Who *are* you, O great mountain? Before Zerubbabel *you shall become* a plain! And he shall bring forth the capstone with shouts of 'Grace, grace to it!'"" (Zechariah 4:6-7). This passage and many others (i.e., Acts 1:8, Ephesians 3:20, etc.) speak of a supernatural empowerment to influence and lead others. As we believe in the Holy Spirit to work through us in our leadership assignments, He will cause us to do what we could never do on our own. Remember, we are not called to lead in our natural strength, but in His strength.

These 25 keys are not something we are going to always feel like doing, nor will they seem convenient to implement, but as we move forward in them, the culture we are leading will increasingly produce world changers.

> Instead of trying to implement each of these 25 keys, we suggest you determine which of the above keys is being highlighted to you and your team, and develop a plan to implement those.

As we close out this chapter on creating a culture of empowerment, let's consider Solomon, one of the greatest empowering leaders in history. The Queen of Sheba had heard about the extraordinary "organization" Solomon was leading, so she decided to see for herself.

"And when the queen of Sheba had seen all the wisdom of Solomon, the house that he had built, the food on his table, the seating of his servants, the service of his waiters and their apparel, his cupbearers, and his entryway by which he went up to the house of the LORD, there was no more spirit in her. Then she said to the king: 'It was a true report which I heard in my own land about your words and your wisdom. However I did not believe the words until I came and saw with my own eyes; and indeed the half was not told me. Your wisdom and prosperity exceed the fame of which I heard. Happy *are* your men and happy *are* these your servants, who stand continually before you *and* hear your wisdom! Blessed be the LORD your God, who delighted in you, setting you on the throne of Israel! Because the LORD has loved Israel forever, therefore He made you king, to do justice and righteousness'" (1 Kings 10:4-9).

This sounds like a truly empowering culture – excellence, success, and happy team members. How did this happen? Certainly Solomon's father, David, created a strong foundation, but Solomon took it to another level through an encounter with God.

"At Gibeon the Lord appeared to Solomon in a dream by night; and God said, 'Ask! What shall I give you' And Solomon said … 'give to Your servant an understanding heart to judge Your people, that I may discern between good and evil. For who is able to judge this great people of Yours?'" (1 Kings 3:5-9). Solomon basically said, "Lord, do something supernatural in me, so that I will be a great leader to the people I am leading." His humility, his integrity, and his desire to treat every person rightly caused grace to flow to him and through him, and the rest is history.

As each of us gets on our knees with a similar prayer to our Father, this grace will also flow to us and many will be blessed because of the heart we have for Him and His people.

WHAT WE ARE NOT SAYING

- We are not saying we will always be interpreted by others as a good leader, even when we are.
- We are not saying to keep the wrong people on our team in our business or organization.
- We are not saying we should invest in all relationships equally.

DECLARATIONS

- My leadership is expressed as 1 Corinthians 13 love, and my teams have healthy attitudes and communication in relationships.
- I inspire people to do what they never thought they could do.
- I am a leader who continually thinks win-win in my relationships.

CHOOSING WHO TO EMPOWER & WHEN

One of our main missions in life is to empower others to become what they never thought they would become. We are called to be influencers.

Steve Backlund

As a child and teen, I participated in sports regularly. I played baseball, football, basketball, and participated some in track and field. As an adult, I continued to play recreational league basketball and softball, plus I spent many years coaching. I started coaching the four and five-year-old soccer league and eventually coached varsity basketball and baseball at the high school level.

I had the privilege of being a coach for my two boys (Joel and Kyle) throughout their childhood and teen years. As they grew older, the Lord made a way for me to be a part of their athletic lives. One of the highlights of those years was when I was the assistant coach on their high school boys' basketball team when they won the Nevada state title for their division (with both my sons starting on the team and making strong contributions to the championship). How sweet that was!

I found my experience in coaching sports really helped me become a more empowering leader. To be a good coach, one needs to:
- **Inspire the team** to sacrifice personal agendas for a greater goal
- Be able to determine what is the **best role for each team member**
- Be able to have **strategic practice sessions** before they play the games
- Take time to **teach the fundamentals** of the sport each year

- Help the players develop **"team chemistry"** together so they enjoy one another and value one another
- Be able to develop a **good plan for each opponent** they play
- Be able to connect with and **motivate different kinds of temperaments** in a way that helps them
- Be able to **make proper adjustments** in the middle of the game to increase the likelihood of winning
- **Trust his or her "gut"** on decision making
- Have the ability to **see undeveloped or underdeveloped talent** in players, which can be strengthened for the player's and team's benefit
- **Determine who has the "hot hand"** and find ways to give him or her more opportunities to impact the game. (Note: The player with the "hot hand" in basketball is the one who is making a lot of baskets in a particular game or part of the season.)

In your specific leadership role, who should you empower to have influence and play a significant role in your group or organization?
- **Someone with whom you have a "God story" for recruiting** – When we ask and trust God for supernatural wisdom in the decisions we are making, He will answer with indications and assurance for whom we should empower. "If any of you lacks wisdom, let him ask of God, who gives to all liberally and without reproach, and it will be given to him" (James 1:5).
- **Someone who is really "with you"** – When filling your most important positions, look first at those who already have buy-in to you as a leader. It is better to take a little less talented person but who has demonstrated an understanding and appreciation of you.
- **Someone who shares your basic core values** – Again, it is better to empower a less gifted person who shares your core values than a gifted person who does not.
- **Someone whom you have "dated" successfully with lower levels of responsibility and influence before "marrying" into placement in a prominent position** – In as many relational situations as possible, this principle will help lessen future organizational relationship breakdowns.
- **Someone you or one of your key leaders has good communication with to help make sure expectations are understood and agreed upon** – Empowerment without training and ongoing relational connection is not true empowerment.
- **Someone who has had the proper training for their role** – This training serves best when it includes: 1) clear job description, 2) watching someone

more experienced in the role, 3) taking over the role with a key person present who is giving feedback, and 4) performing the role with regular meetings with overseer/mentor to strengthen heart connections and to see empowerment truly work.

- **Someone who has the skill set or the developing skill set for their role** – We want a team of excellence. Just because someone is a great person, it does not mean they are to be on your team.
- **Someone who is recommended by people you trust** – It is wise to communicate with past leaders/employers of the person you desire to empower. Even though you don't want to hold people to their past, it is very helpful to know the tendencies they have exhibited in other settings. This information will help determine if you should select them and, if you do, in the initial and ongoing communication with your team member.
- **Someone who has demonstrated emotional intelligence in other places** – We all need to grow in emotional maturity, but we do need to be careful in empowering someone who has major unresolved emotional issues.
- **Someone who does not have ongoing life issues which could regularly interfere with their role and relationship with the team** – It is especially good to have insight on the following important life issues before making a big commitment to a person: 1) physical health, 2) financial situation, 3) family situation (we suggest you interview or get to know the spouse before selections are made for influential positions), and 4) other commitments they have which may make it difficult to bring their full selves to your team.

EMPOWERING PEOPLE BEFORE THEY SEEM READY

Even though we are to be careful to empower people who seem ready for their position, we don't discount the importance of giving people opportunities they don't feel they are ready for. Jesus certainly did this with His disciples. He did not play it safe. His goal was not a "mess free" environment, and neither should ours be. Remember, if our aim is to prevent a Judas, we will probably never have eleven world changers.

So how do we implement wisdom in selecting our team, but still have a "hero incubator" where individuals can soar, do what they never thought they could do, and become great? Here are some ideas on how to make that happen:

- Focus on "keeping your beliefs on" for your team members even when their behavior is challenging those beliefs.

- Address team members' poor beliefs or poor conduct through a prophetic mindset. "Where you are going, you cannot take *that* with you."
- Celebrate and appreciate team members on a regularly basis.
- Expose your team to people and books/teachings that will inspire them to think bigger about what is possible for themselves and the organization.
- Have a good plan to decrease future relational and emotional challenges of team members by having proactive communication (both group and personal).
- Give team members opportunities to play a significant role in helping you and in furthering the goals and influence of the organization.
- Include team members in projects and events you are doing, so they can be with you more than just at group meetings and personal meetings.
- Allow them to influence you in your thinking and in decisions or projects.
- Find ways to share the increase or profit the organization achieves with team members.
- Find ways to have a culture of personal growth, rather than simply a culture of completing projects.

TEN TRAITS TO AVOID WHEN SELECTING TEAM MEMBERS

Here are ten behaviors you may see demonstrated by some people that could develop into challenges in team settings:
1. Regularly complaining or gossiping
2. Overly resistant to change
3. Moody
4. Overly sensitive to correction
5. Prone to negative thinking
6. Easily distracted
7. Making messes on social media through regular unwise comments or posts
8. Time wasters
9. Dishonest
10. Entitled

ADDITIONAL PRACTICAL WISDOM ON CHOOSING WHO TO EMPOWER AND WHEN:

- Empowerment needs to look different for different people. We cannot use a one-size-fits-all approach in motivating and empowering people.
- People need to be empowered at a level that sets them up for success. We want to stretch people into new experiences, but we need to be careful to not stretch them too far too soon.
- Understand the strengths and fears of those on your team.
- Give them smaller things to do in the beginning and see how they do, how they work with you, etc.
- Realize some people have great character, while others may have obvious character issues. When a person has character issues but also has tremendous gifts, find ways for them to have forward movement in their gift. It is much easier to steer (bring change or correction) to something moving – just like steering a moving vehicle is better than steering a parked vehicle.
- Overcome any prejudices that may blind you to people needing to be empowered in your environment, such as racial, gender, economic, and age prejudices.

WHAT WE ARE NOT SAYING

- We are not saying we will never bring someone on our team who has known weaknesses or has people who do not like them.
- We are not saying all people will get equal access to us.
- We are not saying everyone will be empowered at the same level.

DECLARATIONS

- I have incredible insight and wisdom in knowing who to empower, when to empower them, and how much to release them under my influence.
- I am good at maintaining high-level beliefs about my team members even when they disappoint me.
- My goal is not to prevent messes, but to raise up world changers. I am a hero incubator.

CHAPTER
8
INCREASING THE LIKELIHOOD OF BEING EMPOWERED

And Jesus increased in wisdom and stature,
and in favor with God and men.

Luke 2:52

"I t's not fair!" Johnny said to his third grade teacher when she let Abner go out to recess early, but not Johnny. "Miss Jones, you never let me do anything," Johnny sobbed as he threw his book through the class window. Years later, when Johnny was an adult, he was thinking of this scenario when his pastor, Ernie Empowerment, chose Fred Faithful to preach the Good Friday sermon instead of him. "Pastor Empowerment, you don't empower me as you should! Haven't you read Steve Backlund's book *The Culture of Empowerment?* He would certainly say you are an unempowering leader because of how little you empower others and me. You are a controlling leader who has favorites. I am leaving the church. Goodbye!"

Like Johnny, everyone wants to be empowered more. Everyone desires more opportunities to shine.

For over 40 years, I have been empowered by various church and other leaders to have influence in the environments they lead. These leaders would basically say, "Steve, we want you to contribute to our environment by doing this." What a joy and honor it is to be empowered and trusted!

Like all of us, there are limits to how much I have been and am released to do. "Steve, we don't think you are to do this particular thing here." These words are usually not directly spoken, but it is clear that limitations exist on how much I am being empowered. Just like you, I want to have more favor and open doors than I currently have. I wish I could speak to bigger groups. I wish my opinion were more valued in certain situations. Like many people, I am not trusted as much as I would like to be.

In this chapter, we will give you ideas and principles for how to increase the favor in your life. We will help you understand the spiritual laws that will cause others to value you more, and we will share common "favor-busters" to avoid.

HOW CAN WE INCREASE THE LIKELIHOOD OF BEING EMPOWERED BY OUR LEADERS?

When someone favors us, they feel or show approval for us. Favor is a spiritual force that will create opportunities through the relationships we have.

"And Jesus increased in wisdom and stature, and in favor with God and men" (Luke 2:52). Jesus "increased" in His favor. So can we.

Here is a powerful passage from Proverbs: "My son, do not forget my law, but let your heart keep my commands; for length of days and long life and peace they will add to you. Let not mercy and truth forsake you; bind them around your neck, write them on the tablet of your heart, **and so find favor and high esteem in the sight of God and man**" (Proverbs 3:1-4). Those who live a life of godly principles will "find" favor and high esteem from God and people.

The biblical story of Esther also speaks powerfully concerning favor. "So it was, when the king saw **Queen Esther** standing in the court, **that she found favor in [the king's] sight**" (Esther 5:2). God positioned her for an incredible divine purpose to be accomplished.

None of us know what we are being prepared for. This reality increases the wonder in our spiritual journey. Just as Esther's favor saved her people, our favor is a strategic instrument in God's hand to bring freedom and restoration to many.

Know this about favor:
- Most people would like more favor than they have.
- If we focus on doing the right thing instead of trying to make people like us, we will end up with much more favor.
- Our response to situations where we perceive we are not favored will contribute greatly to our level of favor in the future.
- We would be wise to celebrate the favor we do have instead of focusing on the favor we don't seem to have.
- When we let go of expectations that the one we are serving must be the one to favor and empower us, then we increase the likelihood of having a life of increasing favor.

WISDOM TO INCREASE YOUR FAVOR WITH OTHERS
(WHICH WILL INCREASE THE LIKELIHOOD OF YOU BEING EMPOWERED)

Believe you are in the right place – Double-mindedness is the enemy of great influencers. The more convinced we are that we are supposed to be in a job or organization, then the more inner resolve we will have to be empowered. If we don't believe we are to be in a particular place, we will be regularly frustrated by the imperfections of our environment. It will then be difficult for us to be empowered because our leaders will have doubts about our commitment to the organization and to them.

Overcome disappointment – Remember that a common pattern of relationships is this: excitement, disappointment, and then either growth or separation from the relationship. Every assignment and environment has some negatives. Those who proactively address inner disappointment will have a more supportive and forward-moving spirit, thus they will more likely be empowered.

Build trust – One of the most important things we can do in a new assignment is to build trust with our team and our leaders. Trust is the currency of influence. Our favor increases in proportion to how much people trust us. As people observe how we treat others, our attitudes, our competence, our work ethic, and our lifestyle, they will unconsciously determine how much they trust us. It is the wise person who embraces the process of building trust in relationships and organizations.

Buy into the vision of your leader – Bill Johnson (Senior Leader of Bethel

Church, Redding, CA) says he won't buy into your vision until he knows you have bought into his. In other words, you won't be empowered under his leadership if you haven't first had a heart commitment to him and his vision. Bill is basically saying this, "You have many choices in what you could do, and if you believe Bethel is the place you are to primarily release your gifts and influence others through, then your commitment to my vision is a first step to this happening." It is important to understand that the highest level of buy-in is not just an outward acceptance, but one that manifests in excitement about the vision that overflows in communication with others.

Be faithful in small things – "Well *done*, good servant; because you were faithful in a very little, have authority over ten cities" (Luke 19:17). One of the greatest spiritual laws is this: Faithfulness in small things opens the door to greater empowerment. This faithfulness is not simply the act of being consistent in responsibility, but it is, more importantly, what we think while we are doing it. We are "full of faith" and not just acting out of duty. We believe that what we are doing is making a difference, no matter how small it may appear to others and us.

Know things are not always going to be "fair" – "And when they had received *it*, they complained against the landowner, saying, 'These last *men* have worked *only* one hour, and you made them equal to us who have borne the burden and the heat of the day.' But he answered one of them and said, 'Friend, I am doing you no wrong. Did you not agree with me for a denarius? Take *what is yours* and go your way. I wish to give to this last man the *same* as to you'" (Matthew 20:11-14). A culture of empowerment does not focus on giving equal opportunity to everyone for expression, influence, and remuneration, but it focuses on giving everyone equal opportunity to grow into these things.

See current situations as training for where you are going – Prophetic vision for the future tells us we are being prepared for greater influence in the days ahead. As we embrace this, we realize everything in our lives now is training for where we are going. Circumstances now are the opportunity for us to learn how to emotionally respond to challenging situations and relationships. We are being trained how to thrive in diverse kinds of situations. Vision for the future gives purpose for the present.

Be good at asking questions – Those who ask good questions demonstrate a heart to learn and a confidence to engage leaders at a higher level. Leaders tend to be wary of people who don't ask questions because it does not reflect a highly teachable heart, nor does it reflect a heart of really wanting to understand their leader. Also, questions like the following at the beginning of a relationship with a leader are helpful to the future relationship:

- What qualities do your most effective team members have?
- What qualities have past team members had that have caused you the most difficulty for you and the team?
- What will you do if you see something in me you believe needs to be changed?
- What do you want me to do if I have questions or concerns about something you do?

Be teachable – "God resists the proud, but gives grace (empowerment) to the humble" (James 4:6). One component of humility is being teachable. Those who proactively open up for input to advance in work skills, relationship skills, and in integrity will have grace flow to them. Also, we can increase in teachability by asking for feedback: "What could I have done better in how I did that?" or "Is there anything I am missing that is important to you in how I do my job (or ministry assignment)?"

Be an asset – Solve problems. Do your job well and with enthusiasm. Support others in what they do. Improve team morale. Be solution focused instead of problem focused. Exceed expectations, but don't do it to be seen by men, but "whatever you do, do it heartily, as to the Lord and not to men" (Colossians 3:23).

Be a team player – The skill of working well with others is one of the most important attributes a person can bring to a team. Most leaders are going to choose someone with a little less ability who will positively add to a team dynamic, than they would choose someone with greater skills who is self-centered and has poor relational skills.

Learn how to communicate effectively with your leader – Understand how he or she likes to be communicated with. Send "messages" to them indicating you understand what is important to them. If you are unable to meet an expectation, let someone know at the earliest point. Be known to your leader as someone who is a proactive communicator.

Understand your season and assignment – Discern the bigger things happening in your life through your current position that are preparing you for your future. As you put language to this, it will help clarify the season you are in and the assignment you have. For instance you could conclude, "This is a season for me to learn how to thrive inwardly when I feel outwardly under-utilized" or "This is a time when God is teaching me to grow in my administrative skills" or "One of my main assignments in this role is to encourage and support the younger team members."

Celebrate what you have and what you get to do, instead of what you don't have – Leaders tend to not want to empower grumblers because they intuitively know the grumbler is a thermometer in the environment, not a thermostat. Grumblers allow themselves to be empowered by negative things, while the "thermostatic" person finds a way to positively affect the "temperature" in people's lives. These "thermostat people" are already empowering people so they will be given more opportunities to be empowered at a higher level.

Have unique skills your team needs and keep growing in those skills – It is not enough to just be a nice person, but we need to have a growing skill set that helps the organization accomplish its purpose at a higher level.

Be a forward moving person who is zealous for personal growth – Keep growing, even if your leader is not empowering you to the level you want. Don't depend on him or her for you to move forward in life. Find ways to thrive and advance now. In Exodus 14:15, when the Israelites were hemmed in by the Red Sea and the Egyptians, God asked Moses, "Why do you cry to Me? Tell the children of Israel to go forward." As they moved forward, things broke open before them. Hear this: There is a time to pray for breakthrough, but there is also a time not to pray but to focus on what it means to move forward. As we move forward in life, it will dramatically increase the likelihood of being empowered.

Understand and embrace the core values of the organization – Every organization has a unique culture that impacts relationships, priorities, finances, conflict resolution, and other areas. As we understand and live these out, it will increase our ability to take on greater responsibility in that organization. We are not saying we should compromise our core values to "climb the ladder" into positions of authority, but it is wise to seek to discern the unique ways things are done in the teams we are a part of.

Give empowerment to others in your current situation – "Give and it will be given to you" (Luke 6:38). The context of this verse is not about money, but about receiving favor in relationships. "Judge not, and you shall not be judged. Condemn not, and you shall not be condemned. Forgive, and you will be forgiven" (verse 37). It also says, "With the measure you use, it will be measured back to you" (verse 38). One of the best things we can do to be empowered by others in the future is to empower people abundantly now.

EMPOWERMENT BUSTERS

Recognize these empowerment busters that will decrease trust and decrease the likelihood that leaders will want to empower you:

- Not following through on what you say you will do
- Having an entitlement attitude with little or no servant's heart
- Being a reactive, instead of proactive, communicator
- Gossiping or grumbling
- Doing only the minimum
- Lying
- Stealing
- Wasting time
- Performing for approval mindset – trying too hard to not make mistakes or trying too hard to impress leaders
- Being regularly tardy
- Not being a "self starter," but regularly needing to be told what to do
- Displaying moodiness
- Being defensive, unable to admit mistakes, or not able to ask for help
- Having limited skills and abilities
- Being regularly overwhelmed by personal problems
- Having relational boundaries that have become walls hindering good heart connection
- Being self-centered
- Having a slave or servant mentality that is afraid to voice an opinion
- Having a lack of buy-in for corporate vision
- Not being a team player
- Having poor grooming and disheveled appearance
- Making social media "messes"
- Being a chronically high-maintenance individual
- Having your closest friends be people who are negative and non-productive
- Doing unwise things outside of work time that cause a negative reputation

Once we have recognized and taken steps to overcome tendencies in us that may cause others to be hesitant to empower us, we can then move on to get healing from any past hurts that could hinder our relationships with leaders. Although this can happen in many different realms of society, in this chapter we want to speak to those who have had painful experiences in the church.

HEALING FROM HURTFUL RELATIONSHIPS WITH CHURCH LEADERS

Many Christians have had negative experiences with church leaders. Instead of being empowered, they were disempowered and not honored for who they were. These situations cover the spectrum from small irritations to major abuse. Whatever the situation, God's love and power can "heal the brokenhearted" (Isaiah 61:1) to experience hope again, and His love can "restore our soul" (Psalm 23:3) to emotional wholeness.

If this has been the case for you, I would like to repent before you on behalf of any hurt you have experienced from church leaders. I have written a brief letter to you, representing your past church leaders, expressing this repentance, and then asking for your forgiveness. I believe God will use it to bring healing to hearts.

Before I share this letter, I want to clarify that some of the hurts that people believe leaders caused them actually resulted from their own wrong perceptions of what was actually happening. I have been a church leader for many years, and I have had various situations where people accused me of being unloving or controlling, but it was actually not the case at all. These perceptions of me resulted from the person's own unresolved issues, and often from a lack of understanding concerning the many factors church leaders have to consider in making decisions or creating policies. With that said, in other situations I realize I was insensitive to the people around me.

Also, this letter is not meant to be a substitute for any needed personal interaction in dealing with offense and conflict, but for cases where that's not possible, it can provide a powerful step in internal healing and give freedom from past hurts. Even if you're able to meet in person with a leader who has hurt you, going through this forgiveness process will be very beneficial.

Dear Beloved,

I am so sorry that I hurt you.

Please forgive me for not believing in you more, for being insensitive to your needs and feelings, for saying hurtful things, for not apologizing when I was wrong, for sending you the message that you were a failure, for making you not feel valued, for not trusting you, for not hearing your story, for being abusive in any way, for focusing more on what you could do for the church than on how I could help you thrive in every area of life, and for letting my fears and insecurities affect how I treated you. I'm sorry if any of these things caused you to live a life of feeling unsafe under leadership, caused you to believe you must perform well to be loved, caused fear in you, or caused you to be restricted in anyway from being fully you. I regret these things very much. Again, please forgive me.

Love,
Steve Backlund

Now it is your turn. We recommend taking some time with the Lord as you read through this letter. It is a powerful thing to acknowledge your pain with God in remembering the situation, the people involved, and how you felt. Let the words of the letter impact your heart as you read it. If there is forgiveness to release on your part, use the prayer of forgiveness below to help you release it. If you would like to, you can choose to imagine the person standing in front of you to assist in engaging your heart with the process.

Here is a prayer of forgiveness for you to pray concerning past leaders:

_____ *(Say the name of the leader you believe has hurt you in any way), I forgive you for hurts I experienced under your leadership. I release you from my judgments concerning this. I pray that you will be blessed in your relationship with God, in your family, and in your ministry. In Jesus' name, amen.*

After you have completed this forgiveness process, ask God to fill you with His love for this leader. Ask God to reveal to you how He sees that person. Then release a prayer of blessing over them.

We are so thankful when healing takes place through forgiveness. We are also aware that one of the prevalent mindsets that can be established under apparent unempowering leadership is the victim mindset. This mindset believes we are a victim of another's leadership, a victim of their choices, and that our future and destiny is determined by them. We can break free of victim thinking by renewing our minds with the truth. One way to do this is to make biblically-based faith declarations.

Say these declarations aloud:
- I am highly favored (Psalm 5:12).
- I bloom wherever I'm planted (consider the life of Joseph in the Old Testament).
- God makes a way where there seems to be no way for me (Psalm 91).
- God is doing more than I know behind the scenes in my relationship with leaders (Proverbs 21:1).
- I am powerful in my choices (2 Timothy 1:7).
- I have unstoppable hope about my future (Romans 15:13).
- I thrive in every season of my life (Philippians 4:11-13).
- I get excited for what God can do in and through me when unempowering leadership is expressed over me (consider the life of Daniel).

WHAT TO DO IF YOU BELIEVE YOU ARE UNDER A NON-EMPOWERING LEADER:

- **Clarify** through prayer and wise counsel that you are supposed to be under this leader. Remember, double-mindedness is one of the enemies of great influencers.
- **Realize** you will never be under a perfect leader. Jesus was the only perfect leader. (Note – we are not saying you must keep serving an abusive leader.)
- **Identify** what qualities God is developing in you during this season. This is more important in the long term than favorable circumstances or having the highest level of relationship with your leader.
- **Recommit** to being a great blessing and strength to this leader. This is especially needful after the "honeymoon" is over in this assignment. Use your strengths to complement the weaknesses of your leader.
- **Know** others have had difficult relationships with leaders, but still thrived (consider Daniel and Nebuchadnezzar, and David and Saul). They saw their circumstance as a training ground, not a waiting room.

- **Have vision** for your future leadership by realizing how you think and act under your current leader is sowing seeds for how people will think and act under your leadership.
- **Learn** when to communicate and when not to communicate with your leaders about concerns you have. This communication will be the most beneficial to you and your leader when you are able to keep your honor on and when you remain non-defensive.
- **Discern** that how you respond to the faults of the leader over you is one of the signs you are ready for greater leadership and influence yourself.
- **Get input** from a trusted, mature mentor who can help you interpret your current situation from a place of wisdom and experience.
- **Be careful** in who you talk with concerning any frustrations you have. Err on the side of saying too little (especially to fellow team members), but do have a mature mentor you can process your emotions and experiences with.
- **Determine** you are going to increase your ability to relate to and succeed under differing leadership styles.
- **Let go** of the desire to only have perpetually nice people lead you. We are not excusing hurtful words or actions from leaders, but sometimes we need to be addressed with firmness and challenged directly to rise above mediocrity and victim mindsets.

QUESTIONS TO ASK BEFORE YOU START IN A MINISTRY OR ORGANIZATION

Here are questions to ask before starting in a position (which will decrease the likelihood of disappointment because of differing expectations or understandings):
- What expectations beyond the stated job description do I need to know about to be successful here?
- What is your protocol if my performance is not measuring up to your expectations?
- What have been the habits of poor employees in the past that you do not want repeated in me?
- What have been the habits of exceptional employees that you hope are repeated in me?
- What do you want me to do if I ever have concerns about what you and other leaders over me are doing?
- What else do I need to do so you will look like a genius for hiring me?
- How often is there an official review of my performance?

WHAT WE ARE NOT SAYING

- We are not saying leaders are always right and never should be questioned.
- We are not saying people should always stay in an organization that does not empower them.
- We are not saying we should not be concerned if a leader abuses us or others verbally and in other ways, or if the leader manipulates us through constant fear of punishment.
- We are not saying that every perceived problem we have had with a leader is the fault of the leader.
- We are not saying we should easily disregard commitments or automatically abandon relationships with leaders who seem non-empowering.

DECLARATIONS

- I am daily increasing in favor with God and with people.
- I recognize my current situation is the training ground for me to be empowered in greater ways in the future.
- I am an increasingly trustworthy team player who is moving forward in integrity, in enthusiasm, and in the skill sets that benefit my team.

CREATING AN EMPOWERING LEADERSHIP TRANING PROGRAM

The key to being a good mentor is to help people become more of who they already are — not to make them more like you.

Suze Orman

Uery empowering leaders will attract many people who want to volunteer and be interns for them. This is a great opportunity to create a win-win situation for both the volunteer and the leader's organization. This relationship is part of creating an empowering leadership training program.

I have had the privilege of having over fifty interns since I have come to Bethel Church in 2008. It has been one of the best things about my time at this great church. They have been such a blessing to me, and many of them have been launched into significant roles after internship.

As we consider the topic of having a culture for volunteers and interns that is a leadership training program, here is a humorous look at a non-empowering attitude toward bringing interns and volunteers into your organization.

U. Zer Peoples, the CEO of Get the Boss Rich, Inc., was upset about how his interns were doing. He called his secretary into his office to discuss this. "Margaret, I heard some of the interns are complaining again. What are they saying?" Margaret cleared her throat and said, "Well, Mr. Peoples, they are saying they are tired, feel unappreciated and disconnected from you, feel like slaves, and they say you never return their emails and never even smile at them." On hearing this, U. Zer's neck veins started to pop out, and his face reddened as he said, "What! Don't they know how lucky they are to be here? I have no time for that kind of immaturity. If they don't like it, there are many others who would replace them to become our free labor force – I mean interns! Just tell them they are displeasing to God for ever thinking a questioning thought about me."

This is an extreme story to help us see clearly what we don't want to be. I am specifically writing this chapter for my fellow mentors at Bethel Church. Even though my targeted audience is this group, I believe the concepts shared will be helpful to anyone who wants to have empowered interns or volunteers.

I. N. T. E. R. N. S.

Using each letter of the word "interns," here are seven vital directions for mentors to focus on that will help create a successful intern program:

I – INCLUDE THEM

"Then He appointed twelve, that they might be with Him and that He might send them out to preach" (Mark 3:14). Jesus appointed the disciples first to be with Him. The priority of mentorship is to invite the intern into a relationship with you. What they do for you must be secondary to structuring the internship so they can spend time with you (and with those close to you who also carry your core values). Jesus knew more would be "caught" by his disciples through relationship than what was learned through academic-type environments. We too are called to believe we have something good in us that is transferrable, which will be released onto our interns as they spend time with us. This belief will be challenging for some of us to embrace, but it is true. As we adopt the belief that people will be changed when they hang out with us, then people will be changed when they hang out with us.

"That they might be with Him" does not mean the intern will live at your house, but it will shape how the mentorship is structured. The leader will look for every way possible to include the intern in his or her activities such as:
- Participating (as able) in meetings with others
- Coming on ministry trips

- Planning team social events
- Collaborating on projects
- Having question and answer times

N – Need Them

"My soul is exceedingly sorrowful, even to death. Stay here and watch with me." (Matthew 26:38). Jesus needed His interns! We too must be convinced we need ours. Here is a good message to send to them: "God has chosen you to be on my team, not just because you need me but because I also need you."

Gifted mentors have the ability to send these kinds of messages to their interns:
- I need you.
- You are important to what we are doing.
- Your prayers and encouragement are important for where we are going.
- I am so thankful for you.

Practically, we can make intern teams feel needed by:
- Developing a clearly defined role that strengthens a key area of our lives or ministry (and communicate to the intern how it helps us)
- Asking them to give feedback on their experience with us so that next year's internship program is even stronger
- Having them pray over us for particular needs we have
- Asking for their opinion on our projects, the messages we are preparing, and for feedback on things we have recently done

T – Train Them

"And the things that you have heard from me among many witnesses, commit these to faithful men who will be able to teach others also" (Timothy 2:2).

Here are some skills we want interns to have and to grow in:
- Integrity and purity
- Goal setting and time management skills
- Email writing
- Encouragement of others
- Public speaking
- Overcoming discouragement
- Healthy personal finances
- Servanthood

- Leadership
- Proactive communication
- Prophecy
- Healing
- Decision making
- Writing
- Punctuality
- Conflict resolution

In addition to these, there are other skillsets they will need related to their specific role. They certainly will have a measure of these attributes (or they would not have been chosen for the internship), but it is better to not assume they know how to do such things as write emails that have your core values or that they know what you need in their communication to you about the progress of their internship. The wise mentor will spend much time going over expectations (including mini-training sessions as needed) in the first part of the internship. (Note: In the appendix, you can read our "Intern Expectations" that we go over with interns at the beginning of the year.)

After we have done initial training, we make sure the following three areas are continually touched upon throughout year:

1. **Life management** – How can we help them grow in key areas of life (e.g., family, emotions, finances, relationships, decision making, conflict management, etc.) and not just in their specific area of internship?

2. **Beliefs** – As we have learned in this book, what we believe is more important than what we do. Our intern's future will be transformed into what they think today. Help them focus more on the beliefs behind their actions than the actions themselves. What are the lies they believe about themselves? How can we introduce them to more truth? What lies are holding them back? What do they need to believe in order to thrive?

3. **Ministry skills or expertise associated with their specific role** – Give them opportunities to lead meetings, speak to groups, and do other forms of ministry. Debrief with them afterwards in order to help them gain understanding and establish the learning for the future. What was done well? What could be done better? What did we learn? What principle is behind that?

E – EMPOWER THEM

Give them something to have ownership of. Give them a place to influence you and what you are doing. Refrain from micro-managing. Refrain from doing for them what they can do for themselves. Don't work on their problems more than they do. Treat them at the level that you want them to be and call them up to a higher place by believing in them and setting them up for success.

R – REPRODUCE THEM

"… Who will be able to teach others also" (Timothy 2:2). Find ways for them to invest in others. In whatever way possible, have them employ a "work themselves out of a job" mentality. This will probably be most implemented in their setting up the next year's intern(s) for success, but they could also do this through utilizing volunteers or other interns in their role. There are other ways they can reproduce themselves as well, like leading small groups or leading a training time with a skill they have. If you have an intern with a reproducing mindset, it will increase the odds that they will find someone to recommend who can take their intern position the following year (which will make the transition go much smoother).

N – NOTICE THEM

"And let us consider one another in order to stir up love and good works" (Hebrews 10:24). I have a dog named Duncan. He is a black lab, and he always gets excited to see me when I have been away (even if it has been for only a short time). He certainly notices me and gets excited about me. He has not become overly familiar with me, and he is an example of how I want to be with my intern team, my family, my friends, my staff, and others. My goal is to stay enthusiastic about my team and in my most important relationships and to stay as far away from the "familiarity breeds contempt" attitude as possible. Empowering leaders will find ways to consistently communicate with words and body language this message: "I am so glad to see you." Here are some specific ideas on this:
- Notice the good things they are doing and mention this to them and others.
- Make the most of private emails by inserting things like "Here's three things I appreciate about you" from time to time.
- Note when they might not be doing well and inquire (or have a designated team member inquire) about how they are doing.

S — Set Them Up for Success in the Future

Empowering mentors are more concerned about the intern's (or emerging leader's) development under their influence than they are concerned with what they can do for them. Because of this, the wise mentor will take time to discuss the options for the next season of the interns' lives. This discussion will lead to great conversations about decision making, including clarifying their options for their future, finding ways to use your influence to help them, and addressing constraints in their lives that could hinder doors opening for them. Also, it is important to have good conversations about what your relationship will look like in the future so that disappointment becomes less likely. They certainly should always be considered part of your "family," but after the internship, things will shift into much less time being spent together.

More on Creating an Empowering Leadership Training Program:

- Have a "leadership training" mindset, rather than a "help people" mindset.
- Refuse to get your beliefs about people from their past.
- Put resources into staff and team training.
- Model a strong desire for personal growth for your team.
- Expose your team to people of expertise who excel in their same area of emphasis.

Here Are Some Practical Things to Do to Have a Strong Leadership Training Program:

- Have a good selection process.
- Clarify duties.
- Proactively communicate needs, expectations, and desires you both have for the year.
- Determine your meeting schedule — both personal and with the entire intern/volunteer/organization team.
- Plan the following into the schedule: social events, retreats, travel, and other happenings that will bond you with them and with the other team members.

WHAT WE ARE NOT SAYING

- We are not saying all internships should look the same.
- We are not saying a mentor has to have a practically perfect program before having interns.
- We are not saying that in a good internship there will never be cases where interns are not happy with their mentor.

DECLARATIONS

- My default response is to increasingly see the good in people.
- My interns experience exponential personal and team growth under my leadership.
- The people I mentor change the world.

.CHAPTER.
10
EMPOWERING MEETINGS
PART ONE
(SEE CHAPTER 15 FOR PART TWO)

When a leader understands that the purpose of meetings is not simply about getting goals accomplished, but, more importantly, it is about the development of the people in the meeting, then that leader will go to another level in his or her influence and empowerment.

Steve Backlund

One of the greatest ways a leader can empower others is through leading empowering meetings. Unfortunately this is not always the case as the following humorous scenario reveals.

"Oh no, another staff meeting," Perry Perfectionist thought as he sat in the conference room. The meeting started ten minutes late as usual. Perry's boss, Monty Moody, walked in with a scowl on his face and said, "Anyone have anything we should talk about today?" Gary Getterdone said, "At our last meeting there were three things you said we needed to do prior to this meeting to save our company. Are we progressing on those things?" Monty looked perplexed, turned to Dexter Dictation, and said, "Dexter, can you pull up the notes of what we said we needed to do." Dexter searched for five minutes on his computer to find the notes and finally did. "Oh, here they are. No, we have not done anything on these." Monty responded, "Dexter, you always forget to communicate important things to me. If our company goes belly up, I sure hope you are happy for making it happen. Anyone else have something to discuss?" Connie Comfort said, "I don't like having my cubicle next to Dexter because he is always talking to others instead of working." Monty asked, "Dexter, is that true?" Dexter replied, "No, Connie always exaggerates things." As the meeting closed, Monty said, "By the way, I have decided we are going to change our work hours from 8 a.m. to 5 p.m. to the new hours of 6 a.m. to 3 p.m. I've thought about it for the last two days and think it will work best for us." At this point, Gary stood up, shouting, "I cannot do that! Why didn't you talk to us before making this decision?" Monty retorted, "Listen, if you knew how much pressure I was under because of your poor sales performance, then you would realize why I can't bring every little thing to you first. If you don't like it, you can clean out your desk and hit the road. Meeting dismissed."

It would be safe to say this meeting was not a meeting with much empowerment in it. Hopefully none of us have been in meetings like this, but some of us probably have.

I shudder to think of how many meetings I have attended in my lifetime. My life has been filled with board meetings, planning meetings, team meetings, project meetings, church service meetings, small group Bible study meetings, elder team meetings, budget meetings, discipleship meetings, school class meetings, etc. I have led thousands of meetings, and I have been under the leadership of others in many more meetings than I have led. I have been in great meetings, boring meetings, tense meetings, inefficient meetings, life-changing meetings, fun meetings, and even meetings where the leaders or others were abusive in their attitudes or actions.

A meeting is "an assembly or conference of persons for a specific purpose" (dictionary.reference.com). Meetings certainly are necessary to accomplish goals by sharing ideas, planning goals, reviewing progress, and deepening relationships. But when a leader understands the purpose of meetings is not simply about getting goals accomplished, but more importantly it is about the development of the people in the meeting, then that leader will go to another level in his or her influence and empowerment.

How then can we lead meetings that are truly empowering to those attending, while still accomplishing great things? As we consider this, we can all probably draw upon our negative experiences in meetings that tell us what not to do. Let's consider those first.

SOME OF THE CHARACTERISTICS OF NON-EMPOWERING MEETINGS ARE:

- Leaders speaking down to people
- Strong personalities dominate conversation and flow of meeting
- Those attending have little or no ability to influence leader or organization
- Non-leaders are seen more as slaves and servants of the vision, rather than dreamers and co-laborers
- Leaders gives impression their negative attitudes and poor performance result because they are a victim of their low quality team and subordinates
- Little or no proactivity concerning how to involve people in the meeting
- Unclear purpose of meeting
- Little or no action plans developed as the result of meeting
- Regularly forgetting important things from previous meetings
- Little or no focus on the personal or family lives of those in the meeting
- Leaders are insecure, creating intimidation concerning strengths of others in meeting
- Team members are competitive with each other and do not have a vision for the importance of making the team stronger
- People do not feel inspired to come early or on time
- New people are not acknowledged or introduced
- Cram too much into meeting
- Those attending do not feel safe to contribute (and do not feel sure they will be treated with respect and honor if they do)
- Climate of fear created concerning having a different opinion than the leader
- Leaders project an "I have it all together" persona
- Leaders do not create vision for how meeting fits into higher purpose for the organization and for individuals attending
- Leaders do not value people's time
- Surprise announcements made that blindside team members
- Leaders do not anticipate and speak to the anxieties, questions, and concerns of those in the meeting
- Meetings are too predictable with little or no creativity
- Leaders blame subordinates for problems in organization
- Feedback from attendees about their experience in the meeting is never or rarely pursued
- Negative attitudes from team members are allowed to continue
- No recap of previous meetings is done

WHAT WILL BE MISSED IF MEETINGS ARE NON-EMPOWERING:

- Creative thinking for solutions and ideas is shut down
- Ideas that are present remain locked inside the people present
- Leader remains limited to only what he or she can come up with
- There is little to no buy-in from attendees, which means they probably won't give more than is required and won't be eager to give solutions or ideas if they have them
- The power of team is not accessed
- Self-preservation and fear prevent risk
- Leader remains ignorant of team health

Now that we've seen the characteristics and results of non-empowering meetings, let's explore what happens when we move to empowering meetings.

THE MAIN CHARACTERISTICS OF EMPOWERING MEETINGS INCLUDE:

- Proactivity in planning and communication takes place
- Regularly sharing testimonies of successes and wins people have been experiencing
- Attendees are given opportunities to influence the quality of meetings by participating in various aspects of the meeting (e.g., open or close the meeting, share testimonies, facilitate a discussion, lead a team building exercise, etc.)
- There will normally be lots of laughter in the meetings
- Leaders draw out thoughts and ideas from quiet members
- Attendees understand how the meeting fits into the bigger purposes of the relationship or organization
- Leaders are specifically thankful for team members and have a great ability to make people feel valued
- Testimonies of past successes are celebrated
- Individuals are celebrated frequently, including those who are behind the scenes
- Leaders give regular, constructive feedback
- Giving time for people to respond to the question, "Is there any other business we need to cover?"

RESULTS OF EMPOWERING MEETINGS:

Creativity – Creative thinking is cultivated and expressed in a safe environment

Synergy – Drawing on everyone's life experience and giftings exponentially increases the possibility of solutions

Momentum – People have a growing sense they are part of something important and are making significant contributions

Belonging – Because attendees are valued by leaders and team members, they have a greater connectivity in relationships within the team

Perseverance – Attendees have the desire to push through when facing obstacles because they have a big vision for what they are doing

Efficiency – Team members who know they are influential and know their roles will be more focused and prepared for meetings, thus decreasing dysfunctional meetings

WARNING SIGNS YOU ARE MOVING FROM EMPOWERING TO NON-EMPOWERING MEETINGS:

- Belief in and trust for one another is lowering as a team
- Leaders making negative concluding statements about team members (label them) to other leaders and team members
- Proactive communication and proactive planning are declining
- Dominating, negative, or disruptive personalities are being allowed to control the meeting's flow
- Unresolved relationship problems are being allowed to continue
- A lessening of time spent seeking to strengthen the personal lives of the team

WAYS TO BUILD YOUR CONFIDENCE IF YOU FEEL INSECURE IN LEADING EMPOWERING MEETINGS:

- Pursue heart connection with those on the team you feel particularly intimidated by
- Pull on the strengths of supportive team members to help meetings and relationships flow at a high level
- Ask for feedback from your team – find out one thing they like in your

meetings and one way to upgrade them
- Visualize yourself successfully leading a meeting – make declarations over your meetings before they happen, such as: "This will be the most empowering meeting that I've ever led. People will feel valued, ideas will flow easily, and we will get more accomplished than we are planning, on both a practical level and relational level"
- Remember you won't get it perfect each time, but you can learn from past mistakes and celebrate your progress as you grow in leading empowering meetings
- Remember you are the leader – don't be afraid to say no to forceful personalities who want to divert the meeting away from its purpose or core values

Keys To Making Each Of The Following Meetings Empowering:

Staff Or Team Meetings
- Proactivity happens in planning and communication to maximize time and participation
- Agenda is sent in advance to prepare people for what is happening and what they need to contribute so they can prepare and bring their ideas/insights to the table
- Follow-through occurs
- Team members participate and give input with their awareness that not all their suggestions will be implemented
- People's time is valued
- Testimonies are shared and wins/people are celebrated

Church Services
- Leaders believe the people attending want to do the right thing, and their language reflects those beliefs
- People have opportunities to encounter God so they will be empowered by His supernatural power
- Meetings are not seen as religious duty but are times of celebration and equipping to positively affect our families, our workplace, and society
- People are celebrated who are making a difference
- People honor the role of leadership but they also believe they are valuable contributors to the church family

HOME GROUPS

- High level of participation from attendees occurs
- Leader is able to keep group's purpose on track in the meetings
- Leader is raising up other leaders who are influencing the direction and forward movement of the home group
- Leader is proactive in asking people in advance to contribute to the meeting
- Feedback is regularly given highlighting the positive and also giving ideas for improvement
- Introductions of new people are made

ONE ON ONE MEETINGS

- Proactive communication about the meeting is in place and clear agenda is known
- Prepare a few questions, which you send them ahead of time to help get the discussion going
- Remember previous meeting discussion topics (consider keeping an online or paper document for each person you meet with and update it after every meeting to help you remember what was covered)
- Allow them to influence you and the organization's future
- Spend some time on personal things
- Participate in some kind of personal growth experience with this person (reading a book together, etc.)

THE SIX MOST IMPORTANT THINGS TO DO TO MOVE MEETINGS FROM NON-EMPOWERING TO EMPOWERING:

1. Increase proactivity and forethought about meetings
2. Make faith-filled declarations prior to the meeting about what will occur in the time together
3. Meet personally and increase heart connections and understanding with key influencers (negative and positive) who attend meetings
4. Take time in meetings to celebrate people with specific thanksgiving and appreciation
5. Ask the team for their input on how to improve team meetings
6. Deal with your own heart issues so that frustration, anger, disappointment, and low-level beliefs are replaced by attitudes of love and radical beliefs in the team

WHAT WE ARE NOT SAYING

- We are not saying the leader's goal is to make sure everyone is happy in the meeting they are leading.
- We are not saying goals and vision should be sacrificed so that everyone is "heard" in a meeting.
- We are not saying everyone in a meeting should have equal influence in the meeting or in the life of the leader.
- We are not saying there will never be times when a leader must speak directly and firmly to the team.
- We are not saying we should take time to talk to every person in every meeting we are in.

DECLARATIONS

- People feel important and feel safe to contribute in my meetings.
- My meetings create momentum to see our goals achieved and vision realized.
- Because the meetings I lead are so empowering, people get excited to be in them.

EMPOWERING OTHERS THROUGH LISTENING

BY PHIL BACKLUND

One of the most sincere forms of respect is actually listening to what another has to say.

Bryant H. McGill

Have you ever been in a conversation where you found yourself saying more than you planned to? We have probably all had that happen. Why does it happen? The answer is in the power of listening! When we find ourselves being listened to and being understood, we both appreciate it and are likely to say more.

Conversely, we also have likely been in conversations where we have thought, "What's the use? I'll never get a word in edgewise! I am out of here!" When we are not listened to, we usually stop paying attention and turn our focus to other things.

MOST OF US SEEM TO OVERESTIMATE OUR LISTENING ABILITIES

This simple experience contains a powerful truth for the empowering person. Someone who can empower others through effective and supportive listening can develop stronger relationships, encourage more participation, and create a more welcoming climate.

But you, dear reader, might say, "I am a great listener!" Maybe. Maybe not. I routinely ask university classes I teach the question: "How many of you are good listeners?" Usually about two thirds of the class says, "Yes, I'm a good listener." Then I ask, "Thinking of the people you know, what percentage of them would you say are good listeners?" They answer with an average of around 25 percent. Hmmm. That's quite a difference! Is some delusional thinking going on here? The fact is many people think they are good listeners, while many of their friends would not rate them that way. Listening is probably the most personally over-estimated skill in communication!

In this section we will look at how effective listening and responding to others develops empowerment. We will cover the role of listening in relationships, leadership, and effective communication.

WHAT IS THE ROLE OF LISTENING IN EMPOWERING LEADERSHIP?

Listening plays at least two important roles in our communication as a leader:
- First, it is the primary way we receive information from others, and good information is the basis for good decisions in communication. If we don't listen well, we will not take in accurate or complete information. Each of us has likely suffered the consequences of poor listening.
- Second, listening plays a powerful role in relationship development. As we said, people like to be listened to. One of the most impactful tools a parent has is listening to their children, and that begins as soon as a child can talk. One of the greatest compliments a mother or father can receive is for their child to say, "My mom and dad listen to me." Feeling listened to increases motivation, involvement, and self-worth. This is not only true for families, but also for organizations we are a part of. For instance, church attendees who feel like they are listened to will be more involved and more satisfied with their church experience.

As we consider the importance of listening, some would even say that the listener has more influence over the development of a conversation or relationship than the speaker does. With that in mind, do you use listening to develop relationships? How well do you balance out the amount of talking you do with the amount of listening you do?

WHAT IS LISTENING?

Many different definitions of listening exist, but we'll use the one from the International Listening Association (www.listen.org), which defines listening as "the active process of receiving, constructing meaning from, and responding to spoken and/or nonverbal messages."

This definition has some important parts:

- Listening is an ability, and that means all of us can improve that ability.
- Listening involves not just focusing on the words people say, but also on their nonverbal messages as well – tone of voice, eye contact, emotions, etc.
- Listening involves the listener thinking about what the speaker says and trying to determine the most accurate meaning.
- Listening requires a response. The response is very important to the listening process.

As a leader in a communication situation, you first must determine your goal. Is your goal to *give* meaning or to *develop* meaning? If it is to *give* meaning, such as through a sermon or other instruction, the focus is on your ability to develop a meaningful message (appropriate to the audience) and help your audience listen to it. But if your goal is to *develop* meaning (for example, to work with people to solve a problem, to counsel someone, etc.) then the focus is more on your ability to listen and create meaning through empowering others to participate in that creation.

Listening involves our interpretation of nonverbal cues that add to meaning. You listen with your eyes, ears, head, and heart for more than just words. Listening cues can include perceptions of the speaker's vocal pitch and volume, rate of speaking, use of verbal fillers (such as "uh," "um," "okay," "you know," and "like"), facial expression, eye contact, gestures, and posture. Think of it this way: You listen with more than just your ears! Research tells us that spoken words only account for 30 to 35 percent of meaning in communication. The rest is given through nonverbal communication that can only be gathered through visual and interpretive listening.

Finally, listening involves responding in a way that shows the message has been received. When a speaker looks for evidence that he or she has been heard, feedback is expected. This can be as simple as nodding but can also include paraphrasing what the speaker is saying, inferring how they are feeling, and offering an understanding, empathic response. With conscious attention and practice, we can improve our ability to respond in the most appropriate ways in any given situation.

WHAT IS THE ROLE OF LISTENING IN LEADING?

In addition to knowing your goal in listening as a leader, listening can be tied to confidence in leading. **Confident leaders listen better than leaders who lack confidence in themselves**. Insecure leaders are usually less open to new ideas that might be challenging. In a mentoring relationship, one of the most significant indicators of intern or mentee satisfaction with the mentor's communication skills includes his or her empathy and listening. Other people will judge you according to your listening ability, so it would be wise to ask people if you are a good listener.

A good listener must first let the speaker know the message has been received. To do this requires the ability to reflect back, either through a paraphrase or summary of what you heard. The more important the message, the more important it is to reflect this understanding. As a listener, your key rule should be to make sure you understand before you respond.

Listening prompts – Prompts are the encouraging noises and words we use to get the other person to say more. I was on an airplane a few years ago and found myself involved in a conversation with the construction manager of a famous restaurant chain. The man was interested in talking, and for the two-hour flight, I did little but give the man listening prompts such as: "Interesting," "Tell me more," "What happened then?" "How did you feel about that?" and other encouraging comments. I learned a great deal about the man who then wanted to continue the conversation after the plane landed! The use (or non-use) of these prompts can really affect the direction of a conversation.

Empathy – Feeling understood, both in terms of content and emotions, is important to all of us. When you listen effectively, you can reflect on what the other person is thinking or feeling by considering his or her perspective. You place yourself in their shoes, seeing through their eyes, and listening through their ears. Even though your viewpoint may be different or you may not agree with the other person, you try to understand from his or her viewpoint as you listen. Combining this empathy with supportive listening can do much to improve both the accuracy of listening and the quality of the relationship.

EIGHT STUMBLING BLOCKS

Earlier we said listening is probably the most over-estimated personal communication skill. So what mistakes do people make in listening? Below are eight listening stumbling blocks that most of us have seen or experienced (or done ourselves). They are not the result of conscious choices – they usually are things we really don't think about consciously. These eight stumbling blocks are:

1. **Not staying focused on the speaker** – Since many things in communication situations compete for your attention, it is very easy to lose focus. It takes work to keep your attention on a speaker. Check yourself on occasion. Ask yourself, "Am I really paying attention?" "Do I really understand what they are saying?"

2. **Not staying focused on your listening goal** – It is also easy to lose focus on your listening goal. When you listen, try to keep your mind focused on your listening goal (you could be listening for pleasure, in order to empathize, evaluate, counsel, or gather information). Search for areas of interest. Ask yourself, "What am I compelled to do with this message?"

3. **Not eliminating noise and distractions whenever possible** – Noise is anything that impacts your listening behavior. This could include physical or external noise (cell phones, side conversations), physiological noise (like being tired or hungry), and psychological noise (biases or prejudices). It takes energy to pay attention, and we are prone to be easily distracted by other noises.

4. **Daydreaming** – The average person talks at a rate of about 125 to 175 words per minute, but you can listen at a rate of up to 450 words per minute. This means that you think faster than you listen, so it's easy for the brain to attempt to multitask. When you daydream, you come in and out of the listening process, lapsing into fantasy thoughts. Not daydreaming becomes especially difficult when you are not particularly engaged in what the others are saying.

5. **Information overload** – This can also impact your listening. If you have a lot of other topics on your mind or if other people are competing for your attention, it is easy to lose focus.

6. **Jumping to conclusions** – This happens when you think you know what's about to come next. It's easy to make assumptions in order to predict what follows. Once your mind gets moving in a direction, it tends to keep going. Try this test:
   - What do you call a funny story? Joke.
   - What are you when you have no money? Broke.

- What's another word for Coca Cola? Coke.
- What's the white of an egg? Yolk?

No, it's albumen. Were you tricked? Most people are. The brain likes to race ahead, because it thinks it already knows the answer. When you jump to conclusions, it's very possible that you'll miss part of what's being said.

7. **Being too tired** – Sometimes, you're just too tired to listen, and you don't have the liveliness needed to stay with the message. More often, though, a lack of effort can be the result of a belief that you're just not engaged in the topic. You believe it to be dry, repetitive, self-centered, or unimportant, so why bother to listen?

8. **Focusing on the perceived negative attributes of the speaker** – Sometimes you are unable to hear the message when you can't get past different physical, cultural, or ethnic characteristics of your speaker. Have you ever instantaneously judged a person by the way she looks or the accent he has? Have you decided that you can't possibly listen or learn from this person?

Listening takes practice! Awareness of these common mistakes in listening can help prevent you from making them.

WHAT SHOULD YOU DO TO LISTEN EFFECTIVELY?

We covered listening mistakes to avoid, but what should you do? Here are some keys to be an empowering, listening leader:

- **Find areas of interest** – One key to the whole matter of interest is determining how what is being spoken will be useful to cause you mutual support. Whenever you wish to listen efficiently, you ought to say to yourself: "What is she saying that I can use to further support what we are trying to accomplish?" or "What ideas can we work with?"
- **Judge content, not delivery** – Tell yourself, "I'm not interested in his personality or delivery. I want to find out what he knows or needs. Does this person know some things I can learn from?"
- **Ask questions for clarification** – It is silly to sit there in the dark when one or two clarifications could turn the light on. Those questions could be ones directed to yourself (What have I just been told? How does that relate to something that came earlier? Is it similar to something I already know?) or directed at the speaker when ideas lack clarity.

- **Be sure you want to understand people** – At times you may find yourself criticizing another person, saying you do not understand why that person acts that way. But perhaps you're finding it easier not to understand that person. Perhaps you are envious, suspicious, or simply find it easier to dislike that person. As long as you are dominated by negative feelings, you will not understand others. Seek to understand.

- **Hold your fire** – You must learn not to get too excited about a speaker's point until you are certain you understand it. The secret is contained in the principle that you must always withhold evaluation or your response until your comprehension is complete. (Note: We are not saying you should be unresponsive in such things as sermons where you agree with what is being said and you want to encourage what is being said.)

- **Listen for ideas** – Good listeners focus on central ideas and don't get caught up in supporting details or background information.

- **Keep your mind open** – Sometimes we have words or topics we strongly react to that keep us from really listening to them. We must guard against this tendency.

- **Assume the nonverbal pose of a good listener** – If you look like a good listener with an attentive, focused posture, adding head nods, and maintaining good eye contact, then you are more likely to be a good listener.

- **Reflect what you've heard** – Your response should reflect understanding of what the person said before you add your own thoughts.

Remember, you have to prioritize listening. Effective listening is active and requires practice on your part. You have to engage in behaviors that will lead to success. You have to be mentally and physically prepared to receive a message, and you must participate in the active process along with the sender. If you make the effort and take the time to improve your listening ability, you will reap the rewards through having better communication and the people in your life being more empowered!

HOW DO YOU RESPOND?

Acceptance and rejection are the two most basic human feelings. Do I feel accepted by this person, or do I feel rejected? And how strong are those feelings? Where do these feelings come from? Most often they come from how people respond to what we say. As an extension of the listening process, empowering people would be wise to become aware of their own response style and the degree to which it reflects acceptance or rejection.

The two usual terms associated with a leader's response style are *confirming* and *disconfirming* responses. Confirming responses are those that cause people to value themselves as an individual. Confirmation implies recognition of, attention to, and in most cases, a willingness to care about the other person. Disconfirming responses are those that subtly or obviously reject the other person's communication attempts. Disconfirmation implies a denial of the value of the other person.

DISCONFIRMING RESPONSES

Have any of these happened to you when you have talked with another person? How did it make you feel?

- **Impervious response** – When one person fails to acknowledge, even minimally, the other person's communicative attempt. Have you ever said something and no one responded at all?
- **Interrupting response** – When you start to say something, but the other person cuts you off and talks about something else.
- **Irrelevant response** – You say something, but the other person responds in a way that seems unrelated to what you have been saying, or introduces a new topic without warning, apparently disregarding what you said.
- **Tangential response** – When the listener acknowledges your communication, but immediately takes the conversation in another direction. "You went on vacation? Let me tell you about mine!"
- **Impersonal response** – When the listener conducts a monologue, uses speech behavior that appears intellectualized and impersonal, or contains few first-person statements and many clichés.
- **Incoherent response** – When the listener's responses are rambling, confusing, incomplete, and difficult to follow.
- **Incongruous response** – When the listener engages in non-vocal behavior that seems inconsistent with his or her vocal response.

CONFIRMING RESPONSES

How do we empower other people through our responses?

- **Direct acknowledgment** – The listener acknowledges your communication and reacts to it directly and verbally.
- **Agreement about content** – The listener reinforces or supports information or opinions you have expressed.
- **Supportive responses** – The listener expresses understanding of what you said, reassures you, or tries to make you feel better.
- **Clarifying response** – The listener tries to clarify the content of your message or attempts to clarify your feelings. The usual form of a clarifying response is

to develop more information, to encourage you to say more, or to repeat in an inquiring way what was understood.

- **Expression of positive feelings** – The listener describes his or her own positive feelings related to what you said (e.g., "Okay, now I understand what you are saying").

Responding is the second part of the listening process. But here is an important point. The ideas about how to listen and how to respond *all* focus on your role in making the speaker feel supported and empowered. These ideas impact the relationship you have with the speaker and how the speaker feels about you as a listener. This is important to you as an empowering person.

CAN YOU LISTEN TOO WELL?

Much of the preceding sections focus on encouraging and empowering people to contribute, and these ideas work very well with people who are somewhat hesitant about getting involved. But some people need no encouragement to speak, and what if your effective listening strategies work too well, and at least a few people take that opportunity to really over-contribute? What do you do then?

- In chapter 15, we will talk about group norms – the rules and guidelines that guide how a group does its work. One very useful guideline is equality – everyone talks and listens the same amount. In an interpersonal relationship, ideally the amount of listening and speaking each person does should be roughly equal. Obviously there are situations where this idea cannot or should not be followed, but it ought to be a goal to work toward.
- In a group, the leader must be prepared to say, "Okay, I'd like to hear from some people who haven't spoken yet." Control of who speaks is necessary.
- Sometimes, again in small groups, it is helpful to state ahead of time that each speaker will be limited to a certain number of minutes.
- At times it is necessary to interrupt a speaker. Some people tend to over-talk. Empowering them to listen is a critical part of empowering leadership.

SUMMARY

To empower others through listening, leaders must be confident enough to give away some power and let other people talk. To listen well to others, we must suspend our own desire to dominate the conversation, be open to new ideas, and be flexible enough to adapt to new ways of seeing things. As we said, the manner in which a person listens has a great deal to do with how their relationships develop. Empowering leaders use their skill in listening to create the kind of relationships that support their goals for the organization and empower the people they lead.

WHAT WE ARE NOT SAYING

- We are not saying good listening always empowers others.
- We are not saying good listening always improves relationships.
- We are not saying all problems between people can be solved by good listening skills.

DECLARATIONS

- People feel known, seen, and empowered through my listening skills.
- I seek to understand people before I seek to be understood by them.
- My ability to listen at a high level is one of my strongest traits.

EMPOWERING PUBLIC SPEAKING

BY PHIL BACKLUND

*They may forget what you said, but they will
never forget how you made them feel.*

Carl W. Buechner

Every leader speaks in front of people. Sometimes it's in front of one person, sometimes thousands. The leadership role usually requires effective public speaking. And effective public speaking can help you become a leader. While many paths to leadership exist, one very clear path is through this skill. The ability to be competent and comfortable in front of a crowd, engage them, help them think, and bring them closer to you and God physically, psychologically, and spiritually is a wonderful ability, and one not widely shared.

STRATEGIES TO ENHANCE PUBLIC SPEAKING

Effective public speaking is born out of the knowledge of how to develop a compelling message and having the skill to enact that knowledge. Anyone can acquire the knowledge and anyone can acquire the skill. While it is beyond the scope of this book to cover all the topics in effective public speaking, below are some keys to help you grow as a speaker:
- Develop three purposes
- Organize

- Begin effectively
- Connect with your audience
- Control what comes out of your mouth
- Avoid weak language
- Deliver with exaggeration
- Tell stories and use humor
- Transfer learning

DEVELOP THREE PURPOSES

Most public speaking advice suggests you develop a main point – one clear purpose. This is not bad advice, but it is incomplete. A good speaker, one who truly wants to connect with the audience, develops three purposes.

- **Content purpose** – This is the usual main point of the presentation such as "I want to explain how Paul's letter to the Corinthians applies to modern Christianity." That is a nice, clear content purpose.
- **Emotion purpose** – The second purpose is to determine how you want the audience to feel. What emotion do you want to generate in them? Or what emotions (could be more than one at different places in the presentation) do you want them to feel? Are you interested in motivating them? Developing confidence? Increasing empathy toward others? To extend our Paul example, an emotional goal for this topic could be: "I want to increase my audience's confidence that Paul's words are relevant today."
- **Action purpose** – What actions do want your audience to take? An effective speaker thinks about and plans for action on the part of each member of the audience. What kind of follow-through should flow from your comments? Again following our example, you might want your audience to focus on one or two specific points that Paul made and apply them to their own lives.

If any of these are not planned or happen accidentally, your point will lose impact and effectiveness. Think about and plan for all three.

ORGANIZE

Effective organization is the key to so much of public speaking. If you are organized, a lot of other things will fall into place. Here is a basic organizational pattern for an outline that works in most cases:

1. **Develop an introduction** that has these three purposes:
   - Get their attention.

- Relate the topic to your audience.
- Relate the topic to yourself.

2. **Develop the body** in which the first thing you do is clearly state your main point. Tell them in one sentence what the main point is. Then preview the three supporting points. (The preview helps set your audience up for the speech so they know what's coming.) Here is how to preview your points:
   - Identify your first supporting point. Then, use transition sentences to move the audience mentally to the next point. For example, "Now that we have covered the source of the problem, let's move to considering who the problem affects."
   - Identify the second supporting point in the same way you identified the first. Use a transition sentence to your third supporting point.
   - Identify your third point in the same way as the previous two points. Then use a transition sentence to lead into the conclusion, such as "In summary" or "To wrap it up," etc.

3. **Develop a conclusion**, which has three purposes:
   - Summarize and review what you have told them. This will be the third time they will have heard your points, and they will be much more likely to remember them.
   - Include a restatement of the significance of the information.
   - Finish with an action step on the part of the audience.

Study this outline. Study it until you can repeat your own points from memory. Remember, three sub-points have been found to be most effective. People remember groups of three easily. If you organize what you're saying using this pattern, it is likely you'll be more effective. Once you have mastered this pattern, then you can modify it to suit your needs.

BEGIN EFFECTIVELY

A presentation doesn't begin with your first word. It begins the second the audience sees you. At that moment, the audience begins to evaluate you by focusing on your nonverbal behavior. Think about how you might appear to them. Walk to the podium or the speaking spot with purpose and confidence. Move toward the audience before you begin speaking. Begin speaking when you have their attention. Never apologize at the beginning. Look at the audience, scan the room, make eye contact, and begin.

CONNECT WITH YOUR AUDIENCE

Who are you to the audience? To put your relationship to the audience in perspective, imagine this: Hold something up and focus on it, and it alone, for as long as you can. Note when your attention wandered. That is what is happening to your audience. Attention tends to wander quickly. It will wander more quickly if you have not connected with them in the first place. Make eye contact with as many people as you can. Move toward the audience when you can. Use delivery methods to help them be engaged with you.

Also, consider what you are thinking about in relationship to your audience. If you worry about whether or not you are doing a good job and what they think of you, you are making a mistake. **Focus on you seeing the audience, not the audience seeing you.** Where you focus your energy is where your energy goes. Focus your energy on them, and the connection is much more likely to happen. Ask yourself, "Am I connecting with them?" "Do they look like they understand?" "Do they look interested?" "How can I increase their understanding and involvement?" Asking these questions of yourself *while you are speaking* will help you make adjustments necessary to connect with them more completely. This may be challenging to do, but with practice, it comes more easily.

Engage the audience in thinking with you. Give them a problem to mentally solve. They won't be able to help themselves from doing so. Let the audience show you how smart they are, and they will love you. By focusing on the problem, the audience will focus less on you. Thinking together creates a bond between the speaker and the audience.

CONTROL WHAT COMES OUT OF YOUR MOUTH

Speakers who are nervous tend to use filler words such as "um," "uh," "like," and similar sounds and words. Make sure everything you say is something you intend to say. To do that more easily, slow down and put spaces between your words. It is okay to have silence now and then. Silence draws attention to what you just said. **For really important points, pause after you have stated them.** Don't feel as if you need to fill every second with sound. Be as intentional as you can with the words you speak.

AVOID WEAK LANGUAGE

Eliminate weak language. These words add no value to what you say. Weak language only takes up air space. For example, "He was wearing a red shirt" is weak language, whereas "His fire-engine red shirt caught my eye" is much stronger. Again, to help put this in perspective, think about a coffee cup that is only half-filled with great coffee. If you fill it with water, would it taste as good? No, it dilutes the coffee, just as weak language dilutes the message. To develop strong language, paint pictures that evoke emotions. One of the most powerful stories ever written has only six words. Ernest Hemingway wrote: "For sale. Baby shoes. Never worn."

DELIVER WITH ENTHUSIASM

No one will ever be more excited about your message than you are! When you think about your delivery, think about stepping it up a notch. Put more energy into it, more gestures, more movement, more emotion, more changes in facial expressions, more volume, and more variation in inflection and tone. All of these things will draw your audience's attention and engage them at a greater level. Change in delivery is critical; no change encourages the audience's attention to wander. Think about a baseball pitcher who throws the same pitch all the time – that will not be effective! Delivery serves to emphasize, draw attention, develop emotion, and create audience contact. Most speakers, especially inexperienced ones, don't enhance their speaking style in front of an audience. An empowering speaker realizes that to get and keep attention, he or she will often need to intentionally be more demonstrative and expressive. An empowering speaker realizes that planning creativity in his or her delivery style can be just as important as planning content.

TELL STORIES AND USE HUMOR

What memorable stories can you tell? What stories have inspired you? People love to hear stories, and Jesus was a master at this. So many lessons can come out of stories, and people respond to them so well. Begin your presentation with a story. No other words before it. "It was my first day as pastor of this church." You will have them hooked. Good stories usually have conflict, and then people want resolution.

Add humor appropriately as well. Humor is closely related to stories. Humor relaxes people and makes it easier for the audience to connect with the speaker. A famous speaker once said, "Let's just laugh at that!" Humor helps bring perspective to an issue, it tends to encourage positive emotions, and it opens up the heart.

Transfer Learning

This may seem slightly odd here, but an empowering leader views all communication interactions, even interpersonal and small group interactions, as a place where the ideas of effective speaking can apply. Don't just think about these things when you are in front of an audience. Transfer these ideas to every situation you encounter. Of course they won't apply all the time, but you might be surprised by how often you will use these ideas.

Conclusion

As we have said, public speaking skills are one of the most important tools for an empowering leader. Perhaps the primary message here is to focus on the audience, not on yourself. The audience will be thinking about three questions:

- What?
- So what?
- Now what?

Make sure what you say addresses these questions. After all, the important thing is not what you come in with, but what the audience leaves with.

What We Are Not Saying

- We are not saying only good public speakers can be influential people.
- We are not saying everyone will accept your message if you follow these ideas.
- We are not saying public speaking is all you need to know about communication.
- We are not saying that only demonstrative speakers can be effective.

Declarations

- I am an effective, influential public speaker.
- I am comfortable in public speaking, and I have discovered my own unique style of delivery.

- People love to listen to me speak. They feel inspired and can connect with me emotionally.

CREATING A POSITIVE COMMUNICATION CLIMATE

BY PHIL BACKLUND

*Peace is not absence of conflict, it is the ability
to handle conflict by peaceful means.*

Ronald Reagan

Empowering leaders work to create a positive communication climate in their organization. We have talked about many strategies a leader can implement to create a positive climate, but the wise leader is also prepared for relational conflicts. What can be done about these conflicts? We have some ideas.

PREVENT THEM FROM HAPPENING IN THE FIRST PLACE

An elementary teacher we know was asked in a job interview, "What is your classroom discipline plan?" His response was: "I don't have one. I have a classroom communication plan." This teacher had thought through all aspects of his classroom communication climate and therefore didn't need a plan for discipline. There is a good lesson there for all of us.

Here are three things you can do to create a positive communication climate:

1. **Set a pattern for how people treat you and each other** – While people typically have more of a set personality, communication behavior can be moldable. Each of us intentionally or unintentionally teaches those we

influence how to treat others by watching how we communicate with and treat people ourselves. Does my team see me listening well, respecting each team member, controlling my temper, apologizing when I make a mistake, etc.? If so, this is going to help greatly in setting a positive climate. Think about your general style of communication and what your team is likely learning by watching you.

2. **Communicate in an intentional way** – Develop a pattern of communication that emphasizes helping people feel included rather than excluded, focuses on other people rather than themselves, is descriptive rather than evaluative, and is open to change.

3. **Be known as a good listener** – Develop a reputation for acknowledging the contributions of other people, reflecting deep understanding, recognizing people's feelings, and valuing the ideas of others.

These three ideas will help decrease conflict from happening in the first place.

WHERE DO CONFLICTS COME FROM?

Conflicts arise in a relationship when differences happen between two people's perceptions of what is or should be happening – For example, difficulties might arise when I see myself behaving one way, but you think I should be behaving in another. Or when I see you behaving one way, but I think you should be behaving another way. Recognizing these possibilities can be the first step to a conversation that negotiates those differences.

Conflicts can come from differences in how we reach our conclusions – If my experience tells me one thing, and yours tell you another, we are likely to have a conflict. Conflicts come from differences in the meaning of words. Many arguments have come from differences of opinions as to what it means to be a "good Christian."

Conflicts can come from differences over "What do we do now?" – People may agree on what the issue is, but disagree on what to do about it. For example, people may agree that the church needs to more fully address the needs of young people, but disagree on the ways to more fully address those needs.

Conflicts can come from differences in our values – Differences in values related to parenting, helping the poor, politics, etc. can cause conflict. These are often the most difficult conflicts to deal with.

Knowing where the conflict came from can be the first step in resolving it. Empowering leaders help people identify the type of conflict that is happening.

DEALING WITH DISAGREEMENTS

Recognize that in dealing with a disagreement, there is potential for both positive and negative outcomes. Walter Lippman once said, "When everyone thinks alike, no one thinks much." That is a great concept! In any organization, differences of opinion can serve to clear the air, solve problems, open up important issues, and even bring people closer together. Thus, it is possible to disagree with a person without getting mad at them or disliking them.

Disagreements are negative when they:
- Divert energy from more important activities and issues
- Destroy the morale of people or reinforce poor self-concepts
- Polarize groups so they decrease internal cohesiveness and reduce intergroup cooperation
- Deepen differences in values
- Produce irresponsible and regrettable behavior such as name-calling and emotional outbursts

Disagreements are positive when they:
- Open up issues of importance, resulting in clarification
- Result in the solution of problems
- Increase the involvement of individuals in issues of importance to them
- Cause authentic communication to occur
- Serve as a release to pent-up emotion, anxiety, and stress
- Help build cohesiveness among people by sharing the issue, celebrating in its resolution, and learning more about each other
- Help individuals grow personally and apply learning to future situations

An empowering leader helps develop a communication climate that encourages disagreements to be a positive experience for everyone involved.

HOW CONFLICT SHOULD NOT BE DEALT WITH

We all have seen conflicts deteriorate, become destructive, and result in worsening relationships. Usually when that happens, the people involved have followed at least one of the common ineffective ways of dealing with conflict. These are:

- **Avoid the issues and hope they just go away** – Sometimes this actually happens, but usually not. Many people just don't like conflict, so their first response is to avoid it. An empowering leader helps people develop confidence in their conflict resolution skills.

- **Avoid responsibility** – "It's not my job to fix this." When facing a conflict in a church situation, some people say this and assume it is the pastor's job to take care of all the problems in a church. An empowering leader helps other people feel a sense of responsibility for issues that concern them.

- **Avoid the person** – Allowing the issue to become a wall between you and another person is unwise. How many people use the "silent treatment" as a way of dealing with conflict? Too many, and again, this will not solve things. It will just prolong the problem.

- **Get angry and attack the other person** – Some people make anger their first option in conflict. Anger can make the other person either back off completely or get equally angry. Anger is usually not helpful, and a great deal of verbal and physical violence comes from anger that gets out of control.

- **Placate people** – "There is no problem here – everything is okay." This is a way of avoiding the issue. Many organizations have someone who tries to smooth things over without actually solving the problem.

An empowering leader watches for potential or actual conflict and determines the organization's tendencies for how the conflict is dealt with. If the leader recognizes any of these ineffective means of reacting to conflict, then a change is necessary. **To handle a conflict positively, the empowering leader develops a strategy about the situation (whether the conflict involves the leader or not).**

QUESTIONS TO ASK WHEN CONFLICT ARISES

These questions are a way to analyze a situation or help another person think about a conflict during a counseling conversation. These questions can really help focus the conflict and develop ideas on whether or not it should be addressed and then how it might be dealt with:

- How important is it to me to solve this?
- Is it worth the time and effort?
- How have we handled similar disagreements in the past?
- Do I know what I want to achieve?
- Are there underlying, unresolved issues? If so, what are these?
- Do I know anything about the cause of the issue?
    - Is it a difference in our experiences?
    - Do we understand the situation in the same way?
    - Do we understand the issue, but disagree about what should be done?
    - Is it based on insufficient resources (time, money, effort, etc.)?
    - Is it based on different values?
    - Is this situation resulting from differing expectations about roles or our organization's culture?
- Am I aware of how my actions might have contributed to this conflict?

The last question is particularly important. When conflict exists in relationships, each person involved usually contributes something to the problem. It is very rarely just one person's fault.

INCREASING SUCCESS IN CONFLICT RESOLUTION

How can we communicate in a way that increases the likelihood of success in conflict resolution? The empowering leader helps other people think about and develop more skills in handling conflict. The previous section covered topics to think about and this one covers skills.

How can a positive outcome be created? The most fundamental source of a positive outcome is the desire on the part of at least one person **to make the situation better and to improve the relationship**. However, there are times when at least one person in the conflict does not like the other, or communicates in a way that causes disliking. When that happens, it is important for at least one person to focus on helping to take care of the relationship in addition to whatever the content issue was in the first place.

An empowering leader develops his or her own conflict management skills and helps other people develop them as well. Some strategies to consider include:
- Determine to understand the other person's point of view and give it validity.

- Be open to change, and be open to the possibility of being wrong.
- Focus on behaviors, not on your assessment of their character or motives.
- In communicating, attempt to reduce potential defensiveness by: 1) focusing on describing the problem, 2) avoiding evaluation of the other person, 3) being open-minded and flexible, 4) avoiding having a pre-determined solution, 5) whenever possible, treating the other person as an equal, and 6) expressing positive emotions.
- Work through the conversation in these four steps:
    1. Describe how the situation is affecting you, including how you feel.
    2. Describe the ideal. What does it look like if everything works out?
    3. Describe the changes that need to be made to reach that ideal.
    4. Describe consequences that could happen if the problem is not solved.

GUIDELINES FOR CONFLICT CONVERSATIONS

Empowering leaders will model the following guidelines and core values concerning conflict resolution, as well as teach them to their teams:

- **Purpose** – Both people should have the goal of fixing the problem, not assigning blame, hurting, humiliating, or threatening.
- **Timing** – People agree as to when they will work out the solution. (Timing means individual readiness, both psychologically and physically, to invest energy in resolving the conflict.)
- **Commitment** – People agree to stick it out until an equitable solution is found.
- **Place** – Meeting in a place that is comfortable and neutral is best. It should provide privacy and be free of interruptions.
- **Confidentiality** – People agree that whatever happens in the session will remain confidential.
- **Belt-line** – Each person might have points that, if used, would be considered "hitting below the belt." Avoid using these points.
- **Relatedness** – Each person should make an effort to stay on the topic, to avoid bringing up other issues, and to follow the issue through to conclusion.
- **Perception** – Each person agrees to not make assumptions about the other person's motives or intentions, but commits to check perceptions for accuracy.
- **"Gunnysack"** – Issues and problems will not be accumulated, but will be dealt with as they occur.

- **Bad-Mouth** – People agree not to bad-mouth each other before or after the session.

These guidelines (or similar ones) can be shared with staff, interns, volunteers, and church members – anyone who might come into conflict with someone else. People do not like uncertainty, and many people who avoid conflict do so because they do not have the knowledge and skills to effectively deal with it. Guidelines such as these can help people feel more comfortable and confident when dealing with conflict. They work!

RESPONDING TO CRITICISM

Every leader will face some level of criticism. When criticized, some people react defensively, get angry, or withdraw. An empowering leader understands criticism is often a great opportunity for growth, and sees it as constructive rather than destructive. He or she realizes responding to criticism in a positive way is a valuable leadership skill to improve relationships and bring resolution to problems. These leaders also see criticism as a potential opportunity to receive and implement feedback from others.

Below are some suggestions of positive responses to this sample criticism: *"Sometimes I think you don't take me seriously. It seems like everything I say goes in one ear and out the other."*

QUESTIONING RESPONSES

- **Ask for specifics:** "I appreciate your concern. I'd love to hear some examples to give me better understanding."
- **Guess about specifics:** "Are you talking about times this has happened recently, or has it been going on for a while?"
- **Paraphrase the speaker's ideas:** "It sounds like you are upset because you think I'm just humoring you and I don't listen well. Is that what you're saying?"
- **Ask for the consequence of your action:** "How does this make you feel?"
- **Ask for more complaints**: "Is it just this, or is there something else that is upsetting you?"

Agreeing Responses

- **Agree with the truth:** "Well, I suppose you are right. Sometimes I don't pay attention to what you say, mostly when I'm tired or distracted."
- **Agree with the odds:** "I suppose you are probably right. I'm sure I don't always give you my full attention."
- **Agree in principle:** "You are right. The decent thing would be for me to give my attention to you when you're speaking to me. I will work on improving my listening skills."
- **Agree with the perception:** "I can see why you might think that I'm not listening when I say I'll do something and then don't."

These responses do not immediately solve the problem, but any of them will make the person giving you feedback feel more listened to and are likely to reduce the potential emotion in the situation. They work!

Conclusion

We will all face some level of conflict in our churches or organizations, and it doesn't have to be feared – in fact, it might even be welcome! An empowering leader demonstrates effective conflict resolution behaviors and encourages others to develop them as well. Handled well, conflicts can do much to improve the overall growth and development of a team, ministry, or organization.

What We Are Not Saying

- We are not saying all conflicts will be solved under your leadership.
- We are not saying everyone will always get along with everyone else under an empowering leader.
- We are not saying people will always appreciate your efforts to resolve a conflict.

DECLARATIONS

- I help create a culture of healthy relationships and healthy communication.
- I have great skills in conflict management, and I equip my team in this as well.
- I am not afraid of conflict, and I thrive in situations where conflict in relationships needs to be addressed.

EMPOWERING WAYS TO WORK WITH CHALLENGING PEOPLE

BY PHIL BACKLUND

The more others encounter us honoring the boundaries we have set for our lives, the more they will know that they can trust us with their lives.

Danny Silk

I n spite of our best efforts, not everyone will respond well to us. Most of us will at some point encounter people who are acting in unreasonable and challenging ways. The way the leader works with these people can spell success or failure for not only that person but the entire team as well. It is easy to let a person with challenging behavior affect an entire group, diminish the experience for everyone, and reduce the group's effectiveness, but that is not the best way to respond.

Because they can seemingly be impossible to avoid, it may help you to identify some of the different types of challenging people you will likely encounter so you can proactively decide the best way to interact with them. They include:

- **Overly aggressive people** – They tend to bully others. They can be cynical, argumentative, and have difficulty ever believing they are wrong. They can be explosive, bossy, and unwilling to bend to the will of the group. They want their way and will do almost anything to get it.

- **Overly negative people** – They seem to always have something bad to say. They complain, critique, and judge. They also may be overly sensitive, easily offended, and almost impossible to please.

- **Overly egotistical people** – They put their own interests first. They dislike compromise and also are hypersensitive to personal affronts. They tend to think they know it all, often one-up people, and show off. They like to try to impress you, name-drop, and compare.

- **Overly passive people** – They can be aggressively passive, just shy, or even lazy. They usually don't contribute much to conversations or to the people around them. They tend to let others do the hard work.

STRATEGIES FOR WORKING WITH CHALLENGING PEOPLE

What are some of the keys to empowering yourself as a leader in such situations? Below are a number of possible strategies for working with challenging people. Keep in mind that these are general strategies, and not all of the tips may apply to each particular situation.

Exercise empathy – Remember, everyone's behavior makes sense to him or her, even if it doesn't make sense to you. So the first strategy is to try to understand their point of view. This will have two effects. First, by focusing on trying to understand the other person, you are less likely to be emotional about the situation yourself. Second, that reduction of emotion (particularly anger) is likely to reduce the negative emotion on the part of the other person. Achieving empathy widens your perspective on the situation, and this can reduce the possibility of misunderstanding.

Keep your cool – The next option when faced with an unreasonable person is to maintain your composure. The less reactive you are, the more you are likely to use your better judgment to handle the situation. Before you say something you might later regret when you feel angry or upset with someone, take a deep breath and slowly count to ten.

Consider if this issue is worth confronting – Some people or situations in your life are simply not worth tussling with. Your time is limited. Think about whether or not the time and emotional energy necessary to deal with the situation is worth it. Sometimes it's not. It's helpful to remember that people who have challenging qualities also have positive qualities, and empowering people focus on these. Think twice, fight the battles that are truly worth fighting, and focus on the positive.

You make the decision as to how to respond – The other person's behavior is beyond your control, but you get to decide how you will respond and whether or not to engage them. They do not control your behavior and they cannot "make" you do anything. You make your own decisions about your behavior.

Identify the central issue – Rather than react to the situation and the person, focus on identifying the primary issue and on solving the problem. If the other person (and everyone else) sees you focus on the problem rather than the person, you are far more likely get them to focus on the issue too! In every communication situation, two elements are present: the relationship you have with this person, and the issue you are discussing. An empowering leader knows how to separate the person from the issue, and how to reduce focus on judging the person and increase the focus on the issue.

Put the attention on them – A common pattern with people who are being difficult (especially aggressive types) is that they place attention on you to make you feel uncomfortable or inadequate. They can be quick to point out when there is something not right with the way you do things. The focus is consistently on "what's wrong," instead of "how to solve the problem." This type of communication is often intended to dominate and control, rather than to solve problems. If you react defensively, you simply fall into their trap, giving the other person more power. The way to change this dynamic is to put the attention back on the other person, and the easiest way to do so is to ask questions. For example, if this person says, "The idea you wrote is all wrong!" try responding with, "How would you recommend changing it?" If your questions are constructive, you can help reduce their negative influence over you, and at the same time you take the focus off the people and put it on the issue.

Use humor when possible – Humor is a powerful communication tool, and it has been said to be the oil of human relations. It needs to be used appropriately, and sometimes you need to risk the reaction "You think this is funny!?" Sometimes it actually is! If your attitude is light-hearted, chances are other people's attitudes will be too.

Change from following to leading – You may find yourself in the position of unintentionally being led by one of these people. At this point you need to move back into the role as an empowering leader and redirect the conversation away from the topic or person that is being unproductive. If they continue to resist your efforts to do so, you may need to address the behavior directly.

Confront overly aggressive and bullying people with wisdom – Overly aggressive people tend to look for weaknesses, and then go after that weakness. If you remain passive, you make yourself more of a target. When their targets begin to stand up for their rights, the aggressive person will often back down. When confronting bullies, be sure to place yourself in a position where you can safely protect yourself, whether it's standing tall on your own, having other people present to witness and support, or keeping a paper trail of the bully's inappropriate behavior. Not all aggressive people back down when someone stands up to them, so it is important that you pay attention to their reaction to make sure the situation does not escalate.

Examine your own behavior – As we have said earlier, everyone contributes to the outcome of a conversation. If you have a negative interaction with someone, there is a good chance you may have done something that allowed or even caused that outcome. A careful examination of our own role can both reduce the focus (blame) on the other person and give us ideas on how to be more effective.

Talk to allies – If you are not making headway with someone and need to do so, speak with a potential mediator. Sometimes a third party can bring a perspective that you have not seen. Be careful though, and only share these issues with people you trust to handle the information and situation in a mature manner.

Set consequences – One of the most useful abilities is the ability to help someone see the consequences of their own behavior. Many child-raising books talk of "natural and logical consequences." The ability to identify and assert consequences is one of the most important skills we can use to re-direct a difficult person. Many difficult people don't know they are being difficult! As we said earlier, their behavior makes sense to them. A church leader we know regularly uses a good technique. She will sit with the person and first ask how the person wants to be perceived by other people in the church and what his or her goals are. More frequently than not, the person's goals and desired perception is at odds with their behavior. The leader helps the person see this difference, and then suggests behaviors that are more in line with the person's goals. The other aspect of consequences is to take the next step and let the person know what will happen if the behavior doesn't change. Some people need to be told, "Unless this behavior changes, I will have to remove you from the group." Setting and describing consequences can be a very effective way of encouraging challenging people to more carefully examine their own behavior.

Some Final Thoughts

No matter how good you are personally and no matter how harmonious the church or organization is, you will encounter people who seem like they are out only for their own self-interest, who hurt others, or whose immaturity becomes a problem in your environment. The key for an empowering leader is learning some strategies to communicate with these people, learning to minimize their negative impact, and most importantly, helping them develop more both personally and as a productive part of your church or organization. Learning how to handle people who are acting in unreasonable and difficult ways is to truly master the art of communication. As you utilize these skills, you will experience less grief, greater confidence, better relationships, and higher communication prowess. You are on your way to empowering leadership success!

What We Are Not Saying

- We are not saying we should label people, or create our beliefs about them, based on negative past behavior.
- We are not saying we should become negative about people because some people cause problems.
- We are not saying we should handle every challenging person in the same way.

Declarations

- I have an unusual ability to help people grow past negative habit patterns in their lives.
- I am a strong leader who is also very patient with people.
- I embrace seasons of opposition to my leadership as an opportunity to grow in integrity, love, and in wisdom to help people.

.CHAPTER.

15

EMPOWERING MEETINGS PART TWO

BY PHIL BACKLUND

(SEE CHAPTER 10 FOR PART ONE)

People feel empowered in groups and meetings when they feel safe and when they believe their contributions make a difference.

Phil Backlund

INTRODUCTION

Small groups are a common event in life, and more to the point, nearly every church and business has them – committees, boards, prayer groups, etc. Some of these groups are wonderful – we feel active, involved, and can't wait to get to the next meeting. On the other hand, most of us have been in groups where people are unprepared, no particular process is followed, people dislike each other, and the result does not seem worth it. What is the difference? What makes one group or group meeting horrible and another group interesting and satisfying?

As a leader who wants to uplift and empower others (and get things done at the same time), small groups and meetings present a unique opportunity to make this happen. This can be challenging at times, but with the right ideas, it is possible. It may seem that some of the points I make in this chapter are not readily applicable to the type of meetings or small groups you lead or are a part of, but I have found the concepts I share greatly empower people to help all kinds of meetings become more successful.

Before I share on what empowerment looks like in small groups and meetings, let me share a few thoughts on leadership. Certainly eadership is a highly discussed topic, and it has been a joy to add my perspective of almost 50 years of leading and working with leaders to what my brother Steve has shared in this book. My perspective focuses not on the leader but on how the leader can empower other people to make them leaders! Leadership occurs with other people, so my view of leadership is based on the integrated approach to leadership.

Leadership is reciprocal – It is an ongoing process and is defined by the leader, the group members, and the particular situation that the group happens to be experiencing. There is a give-and-take relationship between the leader and the members in which the followers allow themselves to be influenced by the leader and the leader can be influenced by the followers. Leadership doesn't exist without followers. To truly empower members of a group, the leader must be able to be influenced by the group. The leader who says, "It's my way or the highway" or "I always know what is best for the group" will not empower other people.

Leadership is transformational – Leaders can help develop a group vision that members find appealing. This vision motivates and empowers team members to become leaders themselves and influence the outcomes of group tasks. The leader's task is to make the vision clear to the team. It asks them to make the group goals perhaps more important than their own individual goals.

Leadership is cooperative – Empowering leaders use mutual persuasion instead of power and control. Leaders and members mutually influence each other.

With these brief views of leadership, we turn to questions about how a leader can empower others. An empowering leader needs to know and apply ideas such as the following.

WHAT DOES EMPOWERMENT LOOK LIKE IN GROUPS AND MEETINGS?

People feel empowered in groups and meetings when they feel safe and when they believe their contributions make a difference. Let's look at these two ideas more closely.

Every group and meeting has a communication climate. You may have walked into a meeting and thought, "Uh-oh. Things don't look good here." People were tense, there was little conversation, and the leader looked stressed. On the other hand, you have likely come into a meeting where people were happy, chatting, laughing, and at ease. What makes the difference? People fundamentally feel safe in the latter example. They feel safe from personal attacks, safe from uncertainties, and safe from wasting their time. People feel safe to share their ideas, safe to agree or disagree with the ideas of others, and safe to trust the group to get things done.

People also believe they individually can make a difference when the latter type of meeting happens. Have you ever been in a meeting where you thought "What's the use? No one will listen to me. That guy over there runs over everyone's ideas, and I can't get a word in anyway." A person who thinks like that will definitely not feel empowered. On the other hand, if each person believes their contributions are valued, listened to, and respected (though not always agreed with), then they will feel empowered to truly contribute to the group.

So how does an empowering leader create a safe climate where people feel empowered to contribute? **Help people feel more comfortable by responding to initial questions (even if they are not asked).**

When people enter a group or come to a meeting, they have questions in their mind. Some of these questions are subconscious, while others are conscious. These questions lead people to feel a degree of uncertainty, and uncertainty leads to tension. **The more uncertainty a person feels, the less safe they feel.** An empowering leader recognizes the uncertainties people feel, recognizes they have these questions, and helps answer them. Answering the questions helps reduce uncertainty, increases comfort, and will lead to more group participation. Here are the questions people have:

- Who am I in this group? Where do I fit in?
- What do I want from the group? What does the group want from me? Can the group goals be consistent with my goals? What do I have to offer the group?
- Who will control what we do? How will the group be led? How much will I be controlled? How much power and influence do I have?
- How close will we get to each other? How personal will we be? How much can we trust each other? How can we achieve a greater level of trust?
- Who are the other members? Why are they here?
- How much time will I have to spend on outside work? What is expected of

me during meetings?
- I don't feel at ease yet. Will that happen? If so, how?
- What is the group's purpose and how important is this to me?

Not every person will have these questions to the same degree, and not every meeting or group situation will generate these questions, but an effective empowering leader can be on the lookout for these questions and can proactively help members resolve them. With this resolution comes the ability to achieve great things!

WHAT DOES A GROUP OR MEETING FULL OF EMPOWERED PEOPLE LOOK LIKE?

Famous business writer Steven Covey wrote, "Begin with the end in mind" in his book *Seven Habits of Highly Effective People*. As a leader who wants to empower people, what will the group look like if you succeed? The following characteristics are ones to aim for in your meetings. If they are not present in a meeting, then empowerment and contributions will be reduced.

- **Members arrive at the meeting on time or early** – The meeting starts on time and ends on time. Members do not make "leave-taking" motions until the meeting is over.
- **Procedures are clearly understood and agreed upon** – This includes procedures for leadership, interaction, and rewards. We will talk about how this is done in the following section.
- **Members do not ignore contributions of other members** – Each member needs to know the effect of his or her remarks if participation is to improve. When other members do not respond, the speaker cannot know whether the remark was understood, agreed with, disagreed with, or thought of as irrelevant.
- **Members check to make sure they know what a speaker means** – They fully listen to a contribution before they agree or disagree with it. The question "What is it?" precedes the question "How do we feel about it?"
- **Members speak only for themselves** – Each member speaks only for him/herself. No one says. "We think ..."
- **All contributions are viewed as belonging to the group and are to be used or not as the group decides** – This is important. It means people don't argue for "my idea." After you say it, it is not your idea anymore. If you

follow this, it takes ego right out of the conversation.

- **All members participate but in different and complementary ways** – Some members carry out interpersonal functions, while others fulfill task functions. We will develop this more fully in our section on group roles.
- **Members are proactive and want to achieve results** – Whenever the group senses it is having trouble getting work done, it tries to find out why.
- **The group recognizes whatever it does is what it has chosen to do** – No group can avoid making decisions; a group cannot choose whether to decide but only how to decide. An effective group makes decisions openly rather than by default.
- **The group brings conflict into the open and deals with it** – If you find yourself and another group member going out for a cup of coffee after a meeting and complaining about the meeting, then you are violating this principle.

This is a powerful list. As a leader, look for these things, and try to create them within groups you lead. If you do, you will have a healthy, empowered group!

WHAT STEPS WILL GET YOU TO HAVING EMPOWERING GROUPS AND MEETINGS?

We have talked about safety, what kinds of questions people have, and what an empowered group or meeting looks like. To get there, an empowering leader should focus on three things to develop empowerment: goals, roles, and group norms.

Goals – Empowered groups, leaders, and people know what they need to accomplish. It is the leader's job to define or help define what the group or meeting will try to get accomplished. As leadership writer Max de Pree said, "The first responsibility of a leader is to define reality." I agree. Have you ever been in a group where the goal was not clear? Or where people had different ideas of what the goal was? This is not good. The clearer the goal is, the more easily people can be empowered to meet that goal.

Roles – "What do I do here?" is a question everyone in a group will ask to a degree, consciously or subconsciously. Empowering leaders help make each person in the group feel like they have a role in contributing to the success of the group.

People will have a hard time feeling empowered if they don't know what to do. Sometimes roles are task roles (such as reading a scripture in a meeting), sometimes they are helping roles (making sure everyone has a chance to say something), and sometimes they are supportive (bringing information to the meeting). Some roles can be obvious (e.g., it is Phil's role to get to the meeting and set up the room, and it is Steve's role to copy off the agenda and other handouts).

Most group members only perform one or two roles. One of the most valuable empowering tools of leadership is to help a group member expand the ways they can contribute to the group. Making sure people have specific things to do in the group can go a long way in making them feel empowered. Some of these can be subtle, but if a leader can encourage people to perform the following roles, empowerment will result:

- **Initiator-contributor** – Makes suggestions, considers new ways to look at group problems
- **Compromiser** – Tries to find agreements among conflicting points of view and could change own position to help mediate conflict
- **Information seeker** – Focused on finding facts and asking questions
- **Opinion seeker** – Looks for expressions of attitudes and opinions of group members
- **Gatekeeper** – Tries to encourage participation from all group members
- **Information giver** – The expert of the group – provides information based on experience
- **Encourager** – Gives positive feedback to others that results in an increase in group members' self-esteem, excitement to complete the task at hand, and confidence
- **Coordinator** – Finds connections in suggestions and possible solutions and also pulls information together into a coherent whole
- **Standard setter** – Expresses or begins discussion of standards for evaluating the group process or decisions
- **Harmonizer** – Always willing to listen – group members often seek out this person to help soothe nerves, mediate interpersonal conflicts, or solve problems that are not group-related
- **Organizer** – Helps to keep the group organized via scheduling, mapping out courses of action, coordinating efforts, etc.
- **Observer/commentator** – Calls attention to the group's positive and negative characteristics and advocates change when necessary

Look at this list closely. As you can see, these are roles that groups need to get things done. Someone has to initiate, someone has to coordinate, someone has to organize, someone has to follow, etc. These roles are often done by the leader, but not always. In fact, successful groups have these roles distributed among the group members as this means people are more involved and more committed to the group's success. They will feel and be empowered if they have specific roles.

Group Norms – "Norms" is a term that refers to guidelines of suggested behavior for group members. The term comes from the word *normal.* In most groups, norms are not decided on by conversation, but evolve from the interaction of the members. It is helpful, especially in new groups, to spend some time deciding on group norms so everyone is aware of and agrees on them. This empowers people by giving them a clear sense of what is appropriate and what is not. It also helps keep conflict down. When a conflict gets started, someone can say, "We all agreed earlier that we wouldn't make personal attacks." It is easier to meet an expectation if you know what it is. Most groups do not spend time developing norms, but if the time is taken, group empowerment can be greatly increased.

Norms are generally divided into four different types:
1. **Communication/Relationship Norms**
   These guide communication between group members. They cover things such as sharing turns when communicating, how conflicts are handled, how the group members respond to each other, etc. Some examples are below. (Note: These are just a few examples of hundreds of possible norms.)
   - Atmosphere is to be informal and relaxed
   - Members will have the freedom to express opinions, both positive and negative
   - Discussions should respect each person's opinion and each person should be treated in a friendly fashion
   - Members should work to break down communication barriers and reduce fear in communicating
   - Group roles are talked about overtly and assigned when needed
   - Conflicts are to be brought up and discussed openly as soon as they are noticed
   - Overall goal is to develop friendships between group members
2. **Procedural Norms**
   These norms relate to the way in which the group conducts its business and solves problems.
   - Meeting start times and end times should be clear and followed
   - There should be an agenda that guides each meeting
   - There should be time set aside for socializing

- There should be a clear decision-making process – the clearer participants are about how decisions are made (by vote, by consensus, etc.), the easier it will be to make them; important decisions should be summarized at the end of the meeting

3. **Leadership Norms**

These norms guide the way the group is led, not only by the designated leader, but by anyone in the group.
- The leader should be able to keep the group on track
- The leader is responsible for the meeting agenda
- The leader should stimulate enthusiasm and self-leadership abilities within other group members
- The leader should run the group following the agreed upon procedures
- The leader should be a positive model for other group members

4. **Reward Norms**

Reward norms suggest ways the group can pat themselves on the back, reward themselves for good behavior, and help themselves feel good about what they do.
- Give thanks for people's contributions
- Use verbal compliments and praise in assigning and accomplishing tasks
- Use nonverbal reinforcement – give attention, respect, and friendship
- Set aside time to celebrate successes and for social reasons

Norms can be very powerful in developing empowering group members. When people are uncertain about what to do and when to do it, confusion can result. If people know how a group is to be led, what procedures it will follow, how to relate to their fellow group members, and how to have a good time, the group will function at a higher level.

These three concepts (goals, roles, and group norms) done well can be very powerful in developing empowering group members. When people know what they are trying to accomplish, know their own role in working toward those goals, and clearly understand how the group works, their feeling of empowerment will increase.

HOW DO GROUPS COME TOGETHER?

When a new group is formed, the group will go through some generally consistent stages of development. Empowering leaders both watch for these stages and help ensure they are done well.

Forming (Orientation) – This initial stage of a group's experience is characterized by a high uncertainty level. It is the leader's job to help reduce this uncertainty. People can be quiet and uncomfortable as they attempt to understand the group's goals, member personalities, and overall dynamics. There is an absence of norms and an absence of clearly defined roles, so a lot of uncertainty exists about how to behave and what to say. This is characterized by group members: 1) attempting to orient themselves, 2) testing each other and the group boundaries, and 3) creating dependence on the group leader or other group members for support during this uncomfortable time. The most important job for the leader in this stage is to orient members to the group.

Norming (Structure) – This stage happens when the group decides on norms in each of the categories we mentioned earlier – relationships, leadership, procedures, and reward. Done well, group members will become more unified and more organized. The end results of this stage are that roles are clarified and accepted, a feeling of team develops, and information is freely shared among group members.

Storming (Conflict) – This stage occurs as a result of interpersonal struggles and possible lack of clarification. This is where group members share and challenge each other's ideas. This stage requires active leadership on the part of the leader to follow the norms developed earlier and to identify more clearly the group's most important dimensions: goals, roles, relationships, potential barriers, and support. Done well, conflict can clarify the group's procedures, develop greater cohesiveness, and launch the group into the next stage – performing. Conflict need not be feared if the group has the norms and procedures in place to handle it.

Performing (Production) – During this stage, most of the productive work is accomplished. Group roles become flexible and functional, and group energy is channeled into the task. People are getting their jobs done properly, on time, and in coordinated sequence.

An empowering leader helps a new group move through these stages and recognizes when they might need to occur again in ongoing groups. Paying attention to these stages helps a leader empower everyone in the group.

HOW DO YOU LEAD A GOOD MEETING?

Empowering leaders run empowering meetings. However, the leader still is the leader and as such needs to oversee the meeting to allow members to flourish. Here are some very useful ideas for being an effective leader of meetings:

- The meeting must begin and end on time. Do not wait for those members who are late.
- Keep the meeting moving. Interest lags when action lags.
- Speak clearly. If you can't be heard, you can't lead effectively.
- Prevent general chatter. When everyone talks at once, no one can be heard.
- Keep the speaker talking clearly and audibly. Ask the person to repeat if you think everyone has not heard.
- Be prepared for the meeting well in advance. Write out a clear agenda for the meeting and present it to everyone. State the purpose of the meeting at the beginning.
- Learn to synthesize and summarize the group's thoughts and ideas. This is a very important role, as it helps the group understand where it is at and what happens next.
- Sum up what the speaker has said. Not all members will be good at expressing themselves. It is up to you to determine what they have said and whether or not it has been understood.
- Avoid talking to individuals without talking to the group. Side conversations between the chair and members are disruptive, as are side conversations between members.
- Don't argue with the speaker. Ask questions if you disagree. Let the group make the decision. (We want to remind you some of these ideas for leading meetings will not be applicable in your specific situation, but as you understand these concepts, it will cause you to grow as an empowering leader.)
- Remember, you are not there to "wow" them with your great ideas on the topic, but to help the group proceed effectively. Thus your focus should be on the procedures of the group.
- Effectively oversee the communication channels of the group. Make sure everyone has a chance to be heard, and that no one dominates the conversation.
- Be willing to accept the contributions of the members as sincere. It is important to value members' input if you want to continue to receive their insight and empower them.
- Help the group develop goals, norms, and roles, and then use them effectively.

- As a leader, you are serving them. Your group is expecting you to support them in their task.
- Develop the practice of occasionally discussing the group's progress with the group. This helps increase awareness of its progress and takes care of members' feelings.
- Be aware of members' comfort (e.g., temperature, bathroom breaks, water, coffee, etc.).
- Check at the end of the meeting to see if members feel their particular subjects have been covered.
- Thank everyone for coming.

To run a good meeting and to empower others, the leader must relinquish control. The leader must trust the group members. But at the same time, the leader must ensure leadership is not dissolved in the meeting.

Summary

The paradox about this is that in order to empower others, the leader must have more power than them. The leader must first have the power, and then understand how to give it away. A leader must know how groups work and be highly skilled at communication, at group problem solving, at encouraging others, and many other points. Few things feel better than when we are in a group or meeting that really works.

What We Are Not Saying

- We are not saying all decisions can easily be made by following these steps.
- We are not saying all people will respond well to your leadership.
- We are not saying things will always run smoothly by applying these techniques.

DECLARATIONS

- I understand my role in every meeting I attend.
- I intentionally empower others to identify and function in a vital contributing role in the meetings I lead.
- The meetings I lead are both fun and extremely productive.

Appendix A

Practical Steps to Grow as an Empowering Leader

Every person has the potential to be a great leader, and it's important that we have abounding hope that we can be empowering people and leaders (as well as raise others up in this). We hope this book has filled you with inspiration, ideas, and strategies for ways to move forward in creating and walking in the culture of empowerment.

Here are some key points to remember:

- **Know you don't need to be a recognized leader to create culture** – We can create it wherever we are.
- **Realize empowerment isn't just about doing something; it's about being something** – We cannot be an empowering leader without being an empowering person. We have people above us, people beside us, and people we pour into. All of these relationships have the potential to be empowering.
- **Pursue these characteristics of an empowering culture** – It is encouraging, creates "win-win" situations, has dreamers (not just slaves), has consistent life-giving feedback, makes humor and laughter a priority, cares for the whole person, communicates proactively and consistently, is full of integrity, and creates buy-in to the leader's vision.
- **Value building trust in the eyes of others** – Some ways to do this are to have great follow-through and do what you say you will do, demonstrate vulnerability at an appropriate level, and create a safe environment for your team to bring their ideas and thoughts to the table. Celebrate people when they are vulnerable and when they step out with ideas, whether you use the idea or not.
- **Prioritize listening** – This is a huge key to having empowering relationships.
- **Have high-level beliefs about people** – How we see people greatly affects

how we interact with them, so it's important to look for the best in people, see the greatness within them, and call that out. Speak to them as though they already are who they were created to be (like the angel spoke to Gideon).

- **Publicly recognize the good qualities and actions of your team** – This will encourage individuals and help team members see each other in a stronger way.
- **Appreciate people and be interested in their lives beyond what they do for the organization** – Take interest in people not just for what they do, but for who they are.

EMPOWERING PEOPLE TRAIN THEIR TEAM WELL

We have included several resources in Appendix C that we've created to help us train and set our team up for success in many areas of their lives. In addition to these resources, here are other keys to being an empowering leader:

- **Learn two or three things that make the people in your life come alive** (e.g., ask them what's beautiful to them, what they love to do, if money and time were not an issue what they would do, etc.). Also take time to ask about their personal lives.
- **Have connection times** such as annual retreats, quarterly luncheons, and an annual Christmas party. Having time solely for connection helps build relationships at a deeper level and conveys to your staff or team that they are important to you.
- **Have a high value for face-to-face time with people you're leading**. This time is very important for building trust, fostering heart connection, and deepening relationship. Much can be communicated via email and text, but it's key to have time with your team in person. If your team or organization is large, you won't be able to meet in this way with every person, but you can take advantage of even the briefest of moments with people to express value and love to them.
- **Make relationships an important part of your schedule**. Determine who you need to meet with and how often. Give these individuals permission to communicate with you to help you prioritize it if it has not been happening. It's important to set realistic expectations with this in order to help avoid disappointment from those who want more time than you can give. (Note: We're not saying that your staff/team has unlimited access to you. You need to have good boundaries with your time and know what your priorities are.)

- **Empower the people you're leading to co-create the details of your meeting times together**. This creates a greater value for meetings for both of you. The more you communicate in advance about meeting times together, the more powerful the time will be.
- **Ask your team about their workspace and role**. What's working for them? What could be improved and help them function better?
- **Create opportunities for them to use their gifts and to be stretched into new skillsets**. Give them opportunities to lead and responsibilities for planning, and let them oversee jobs when appropriate or collaborate together with you and other leaders on projects being done.
- **Remember to teach them basic things about their roles**, including orienting them to the facilities available. Have them trained on how to use the printer, copier, phone system, etc., and let them know the things they have access to such as a coffee maker and refrigerator. Make sure they know where to find phone numbers they may need and what resources are available.
- **Introduce them to fellow staff/volunteers** that work in the same department or that they will be interacting with regularly.
- **Prepare documentation so they can easily step into their role**. Have files organized, records available, provide them with a training manual, and give them the history of the organization or department.
- **Give them access to you** via email, phone, and text messaging, and let them know what your preferred method of communication is for both standard communication and urgent matters.
- **Verbally say what you might think is obvious during the training phase**. It takes time for team members to "learn" their leaders.
- **In addition to practical things, prioritize training people in mindsets and relational skills**. Spend time on teaching communication techniques, conflict resolution strategies, and share your plan for having regular feedback.
- **Empower them to take ownership for your team to fully learn what they don't understand**. Although it is important for you to give proper training, you can also let them know it's their responsibility to let you know if they don't understand something, need more information, have questions, etc.
- **Take care of yourself**. Prioritize time with God, your family, your physical, emotional, and spiritual health, and getting rest. Not only is it important to set this example for your team, you will also be able to lead more effectively if you keep yourself filled up.

Appendix B

Testimonies of Steve's Mentoring

Here are testimonies from some people who have been under Steve's leadership. He has impacted many more lives, but this will reveal some of the fruit of being an empowering person and leader. We hope it inspires you to keep moving forward on your own journey of empowerment.

Eric Johnson: In 2002 I was serving underneath Danny and Sheri Silk as an associate pastor in Weaverville, CA at Mountain Chapel. Danny and Sheri were in the process of leaving to go on staff at Bethel Church. Our new incoming pastors were Steve and Wendy Backlund. I had met them several years before but didn't know them very well at this point. As you can imagine, I was a little curious about how this transition would work for myself and the church family.

The first day Steve came into the office, I said, "Steve, I want you to know that I am here to serve you and your vision." Little did I know that the next three years of my life would be deeply impacted by this man. His intentionality in leading and developing me as a leader was priceless. I often draw from those three years in the present as I am now leading and pastoring Bethel. He had high beliefs in me as a person and a leader. Every interaction was thought out and important to him. It was felt and tangible. It was as if he didn't waste a moment or any of our time. He was very intentional in developing and empowering me.

Jared Neusch: Joining Steve Backlund's intern team in 2010, I was a cautious, shy guy who often found himself concerned with how other people might view my words and actions. I was pleasantly surprised to discover the rumors were true about Steve's leadership style and ability. Immediately Steve chose to look past what his experience might have told him about my personality and leadership. Instead, he focused on my prophetic potential and consistently told me about it. Well before the desire had ever reached my heart or mind, Steve was calling me a revivalist teacher. This couldn't have been further from my experience, or even my desire! However, the more I absorbed Steve's encouragement in my life, the more confident I became in who God had made me to be. Under Steve I learned the fruit of this truth: High-level leaders have high-level beliefs about their people.

Julie Mustard: Everyone needs someone who believes in you more than you believe in yourself. They push you to be the fullest version of yourself, ask great questions, and give guidance along the way. In a culture of empowerment, this mentor creates space for you and gives you access to a platform you could never have reached on your own. Steve Backlund has been all of this and more in the few short years I have known him. As our relationship has transitioned through different stages – teacher, mentor, role model, boss, father, friend, and now colleague, I have been strengthened and challenged by him. He is relentless in his belief about me and sees things in me I have not even seen ... yet. But that is what a good father does – he gives you vision for something more and paves a path to belief with words of life. Being so empowering has a cost, and I have seen Steve navigate that cost without wavering. Steve Backlund is a treasured voice in my life and a model of empowerment without an agenda.

Anne Ballard: My third year of BSSM spent under Steve's leadership was one of the most impactful, course-altering times of my life. Steve has a way of drawing out people's strengths, stretching them, and growing them, and then believing in them in a way that makes them feel unstoppable. When I interviewed to intern with Steve, I remember telling him I didn't know what I was called to. He assured me I would at the end of a year with him. He was right. My mind was overhauled by his message of joy, hope, truth, renewing the mind, and the power of declarations. My heart was wrecked by his love for and belief in me. I made mistakes while working for him, but the grace with which he handled them, loved me, and sought to still champion me changed how I would handle others' mistakes in my own life. As the oldest intern on my team, surrounded by others who had already developed their own ministry, at times I felt intimidated. I knew that I was called to ministry, but I knew that mine would look different than those around me. Steve gave me the confidence to know that was okay. After my internship ended, I started my own business of Kingdom jewelry focused on identity words and prophetic declarations. I know this is part of my destiny, and it is wonderful. I can wholeheartedly say that without my time with Steve, I would not be the person I am today. I am changed forever in the most glorious way, more sure of who God created me to be, and more equipped to love and empower others in my life.

Jaz Jacob: Steve has empowered me not only in practical ways of leadership, but also in my ability to flow with the Holy Spirit and hear what God is doing in each service and meeting. When I was serving under Steve's ministry, he would frequently share something at a service or meeting and ask me to be aware during the service what the Lord might be saying. At the end of the meeting, he would then pass the baton onto me so I could help the congregation press into what God was doing. This has equipped me incredibly because now, years after being under Steve's leadership, I'm so aware of what God is doing in a room and in a service that I can walk away knowing we were able to follow the wind of the Spirit and love each person as Jesus would.

Jesse Cupp: Steve Backlund has been the most amazing example of a spiritual father to me, as well as to everyone else I know who has been mentored by him. From the moment I met him, he has made me feel believed in, and helped me believe I can accomplish all I set my heart to. There have been so many times when I've felt a little deflated in my confidence level about being a great leader, and when I leave a meeting with him, I feel like I could take on the world. Even in my weakness and failures, he has made me feel like a victor and like those things were just setting me up to be a better leader because I found my way through them.

When I went into my internship with Steve, I had a dream of doing itinerant (travel) ministry to bring revival to hungry churches. In the very first week of being with him, I got to travel with him and get on-the-job training. After that week, I was already stepping into itinerant ministry. Steve doesn't surround himself with people so they can make him a better leader. He surrounds himself with people who he can help make into great leaders. He multiplies his influence by multiplying great leaders and trusting and believing in them. Being under Steve's influence, I literally feel like I have been launched ten years ahead on my journey into the potential I am called to. Why? Because he is a good father who believes in his spiritual children so much that he releases them into their own greatness. He has redeemed what leadership should look like in the Kingdom of God.

Chris Overstreet: Steve is one of a kind. I had the honor one summer to intern for Steve while he pastored Mountain Chapel in Weaverville. God used Steve to help shape the evangelist I am today by empowering me to speak the word of God over my life. God also used Steve to speak into areas in my life that needed to be developed. Steve discovered that I did not know how to use a computer, so he challenged me to learn how to use one and start to type. He said I might be writing books one day. Today I am a published author, and that has a lot to do with Steve seeing something in me that I did not see in myself.

Steve also encouraged me regarding finances. He told me I was good with money, and at the time that felt so far from the truth. But as I meditated on his encouragement, I noticed breakthrough occurring in my mind regarding thoughts I had about money. Steve helped shift a false mindset I had that kept me prisoner when it came to money. Since Steve gave me that word a few years back, my wife and I have been able to pay off $65,000 in debt. Steve, thank you so much for being a father and a friend to so many people! Your impact is spreading around the globe!

Heidi Anderson: Steve is the most empowering leader I have ever served under. His belief that everyone is valuable and has something to contribute to the Body of Christ has impacted my life in a profound way. During times of extensive travel with him during my internship, I discovered far more about myself and what my gifts were simply because he gave me space to grow. The key Steve holds is that he continually communicates to people their prophetic destiny instead of seeing them as they currently are, which in turn causes people to believe in themselves and grow into their God-given potential. Serving under Steve was simply a launching pad into my future where I was able to take what I learned and create a culture of empowerment around me. People that minister or travel with me today often give feedback of how impacted they were because they felt valued and that they had a voice. I tell them it is because I had the most empowering mentor on the planet.

Matt King: I am indebted to Steve for his belief in and empowerment of me. Steve has astonished me with his recognition and calling out of the anointing and gifting that God has placed upon me. Even if weeks pass by between conversations, I know for sure that at our next interaction I am going to experience some kind of encouragement from him. He knows me after the Spirit, and has consistently called out who I am in Christ. I can recall being a member of his small ministry team on a trip to Texas. He consistently entrusted to me the healing ministry time at different churches. He recognized a grace on my life and empowered me to step into my calling as a minster of God's healing power.

Slindile Baloyi: Steve has a unique style of leadership. During my time under his leadership I was impacted by these five qualities that continue to help me as a leader: 1) The ability to expose his team to senior leaders through servanthood; 2) Belief equals investment. When a leader believes in you the way Steve does, it naturally motivates you to invest in him and his ministry; 3) Vulnerability and transparency are important. My internship year under Steve's leadership opened my eyes to how real, approachable, and authentic Steve is as a minister, father, and friend. His leadership style is motivated by love; 4) One of my favorite Steve quotes is this: "Trust is the commodity of great influencers." Steve's trust in my gifts, talents, and abilities made me feel safe and known. It broke off all limits. Trust equals no limits; 5) Passion is contagious! Whether I wanted my mind renewed or not, Steve's passion for his message impacted my life more than I realized. Steve has the kind of passion that transforms whole communities. As a business owner I have implemented these values in my own life. Thank you, Steve, for empowering me to be a great leader.

Candice Ross: I had the honor of interning under Steve's leadership. Looking back, one of the biggest things I learned from Steve was the power to be victorious in the choices I make over my feelings and thoughts. It's so easy for our human nature to remain in a negative rut throughout times of struggle, but in the midst of my struggle I can choose to be joyful, I can choose to be hopeful and I can choose to be an encouragement to someone in need. When I choose to be intentional and declare life in the midst of feeling defeated, it produces an excitement that God is bigger than what I can see in the natural and, in return, renews my mind to the victory that is Christ Jesus!

Sally Schwendenmann: One of my best Steve moments was when we went to Mexico in 2014 and he said we were speaking to a congregation of over 2,000 people (not 100 or less like I was thinking)! I thought, "I am not ready for this" and although he saw the doubt in my eyes, he said it was a leadership conference. He said, "Sally, they are going to get an explosion of God's wonder and joy when you speak!" I was so humbled and overjoyed that Steve saw something greater in me than I did. He told me that I carry wonder and love, and I inspired him. I later thought, "I actually inspired a leader that has led and changed nations of people, and it's awesome that little me could inspire him!"

Libby Gordon: I affectionately call Steve the belief's body builder. This couldn't be closer to the truth. I was traveling with Steve and his team on a ministry trip and my life transformed radically. I saw first-hand that Steve modeled a leadership where not only was he powerful, hopeful, and refreshed "under the anointing," but there was no "off switch." This was his everyday life. What impacted me even more was that it wasn't just him – it was his entire team. The men and women who Steve has discipled are a testament to his empowering leadership in itself.

Steve has always chosen to take a longer road to his destination because he included others in his journey. He is so convinced of the victorious nature of God that he liberally takes risks to see those around him empowered. This is what he did with my husband and me. In the model of ministry I see in the life of Jesus, He moved in unswerving hope as well as power. Fulfilling all His Father had asked Him included empowering His disciples to not simply maintain, but to do "greater works." Steve is intentional. He sat with me on many occasions and helped me not only move forward, but taught me how to think when making decisions. It was one of the most redeeming moments I have had with a leader when I realized he had no ulterior motive or agenda other than to see me step into the fullness of my destiny. I have no doubt that Steve's catalytic mentorship has brought me to a place of promotion I would not have walked into had I not learned from his example and been under the covering of a leader who had unreasonable belief in my husband and me and made that known time and time again.

Melissa Amato: Steve is the most empowering person I know aside from Jesus. He sees people, loves people, trusts people, and always believes the best about them. He champions people and calls them to be who God created them to be. The first day I went on a ministry trip with him as a BSSM Second Year student, he asked me what I wanted to be known for 20 years from now. I told him I wanted to be known for loving well and releasing God encounters, bringing entire rooms of people into an encounter with God's love. When he introduced me that evening during ministry time, he said, "This is Melissa and she releases God's love to everyone she meets. She brings entire rooms into encounters with God's love." I felt the grace fall on me immediately to walk in what I had hoped to walk in 20 years later. He believed in me more than I believed in myself, and that gave me the confidence to believe in myself at a higher level. My life was forever changed in that moment, and I knew the best decision I could make was to serve Steve. I'm forever grateful for how he has changed, and is still changing, my life and the lives of countless others for the better. He truly loves and champions people well. I'll never be the same again.

Appendix C

Intern/Volunteer Team Resources

Intern Expectations

This is material that will be especially helpful for the mentors at my (Steve's) home church – Bethel Church. But many of the concepts will be helpful to leaders/ mentors in other environments as well.

In addition to the obvious things related to fulfilling responsibilities, here are some of our basic expectations of our interns:

Be a good team player – A good team player knows how to give and take and make sacrifices for the good of the team when necessary. Be aware of what's happening with the team and not only focused on "your world."

Have a high buy-in to the Backlund's message (and an ongoing pursuit to get it in your life) – Be intentional about getting the message in you both on an individual and team level.

Laugh a lot – Hahahahaha! Don't take yourself too seriously and remember that to laugh, you might have to let go of something (frustration, self-pity, anger, etc.).

Avoid making messes or poor choices on Facebook, at parties, how you dress, etc. – Remember you are representing Steve, Wendy, and our staff team. We don't have legalistic "rules" on matters like these, but you have more influence than you know. If messes are made, communication is important. We will talk more about this as a team.

Be a strong encourager of others – We are called to be Kingdom encouragers and our team is called to be great encouragers of other people. Find the gold in people, call it out, and believe the best about everyone you meet.

Have other spiritual fathers and mothers in your life besides Steve and our team – Steve's relationship with you is to be an important part of your spiritual fathering plan, but he will not be able to meet all your needs in that area. None of the mentors on our team are able to fully fulfill that need. It is vital that you have other spiritual moms and dads to draw from. As far as connection with us, we will plan to meet as a team every week. One on one meeting frequency will vary depending on your mentor. Realize that as you travel with Steve (and Melissa), we will try to maximize these times for our relationship.

Travel with Steve on ministry trips two to three times during the year – We will be discussing this in one of our early meetings.

Leading teams while traveling – When you travel with Steve, a team leader will be designated. All of you will do this at least once throughout the year. This will be discussed in more detail during a future team meeting.

Pursue personal growth – Make a plan for personal growth that includes dreams, desires, and goals. Read leadership articles, books, or listen to podcasts that put you on a path to growing into becoming a more well-rounded person and leader. We will have team personal growth assignments as well.

Global Legacy events – Interns are expected to volunteer for the GL booth at conferences and to be available for additional GL needs throughout the year. Please leave extra space in your calendar during conferences and especially during the Leaders Advance in the fall and spring. Not saying yes to too many outside things will help you be available when needed.

Intern teaching sessions – You will each be doing a one-hour teaching/ministry session for the Church Leadership class students in the spring semester (the class Steve teaches). We will have some training and practice times for these to help set you up for success. The students will be invited to your session, and you can invite others as well.

Ignite meetings – All interns are welcome to attend these meetings and to contribute to some of the projects in the Backlund's world.

Be you – We chose you because you are you. We don't want a team of "yes" people. We value people who are authentic and bring themselves to the table. Also remember not to compare your intern role with another role. You were divinely placed in your role for a reason.

Be a student of Steve – Much wisdom can be gleaned from Steve. Pull on him this year, and watch how he does life and navigates things. This alone will bring great growth to your life.

Communicate with Steve and Melissa – We don't know what is happening in your life and intern world unless you tell us. If you need clarification or there's something we can do to help make your internship a better experience, let us know. Please be proactive in communicating with us, and lean toward over-communicating, rather than under-communicating. We will let you know if you are communicating too much.

INTERN TRANSITION SURVEY

Our interns fill this out after their first month of internship with us so we can help make the transition into our internship better each year.

Please complete these questions regarding your handover experience and transition into Third Year.

What would have been helpful for you to know in the general transition from Second Year to Third Year?

What would have been helpful for you to know/understand coming into the internship?

What are any unanswered questions you had moving into this internship (if applicable)?

How could Steve and Melissa (and your mentor if not Steve or Melissa) improve your experience as a new intern on the team and/or have better set you up for success in your intern role?

What are the areas you are doing well in relating to your internship?

What areas have you already grown in since beginning your internship?

In what areas do you recognize continued room for growth at this point?

END OF YEAR FEEDBACK QUESTIONNAIRE

This is given to interns after their internship year is completed to help us upgrade our internship each year.

This information will help Steve and Melissa take the Backlund internship to higher levels next year, so your feedback is incredibly important to us! *Please note that we would like feedback from the entire team on both Steve and Melissa as they oversee the team together.*

Knowing what you know now, if you could write a letter to yourself at the beginning of your internship, what advice would you give yourself?

How could Steve improve your experience as an intern on the Backlund team?

How could Melissa improve your experience?

What would you have liked to see done differently by a) Your mentor (if not Steve or Melissa), b) Steve, and c) Melissa?
What would you like your mentor to do more of and less of?

What worked and what didn't work in your internship?

What keys would you recommend to empower the incoming intern in your role (if applicable)? Do you have training material prepared for them?

What was your most significant personal breakthrough this year? How did this breakthrough come?

How would you recommend improving connection within the Backlund Team?

Do you have any other feedback?

Ideas/suggestions on how to upgrade:
- Church leadership class

- Church leadership class church services
- Ministry trips
- Intern meetings
- Ignite project meetings
- Team social events
- Intern teaching times

Please place the following components of the Backlund Internship in order from most meaningful to least meaningful:

- Team Backlund intern meetings
- One on ones with your mentor
- Third Year corporate meetings at Twin View
- Internship modules
- Team Backlund intern teaching assignment
- Reading Steve's books
- Team Backlund personal growth goals (Minute with Maxwell, reading The New Testament, etc.)
- Participating in Second Year church leadership class
- Overseeing a Second Year church leadership class church group
- Traveling with Steve and/or Melissa
- Global Legacy components (GL intern meetings, volunteering, video conferences, etc.)
- Weekly emails

INTERN PERSONAL GROWTH LIST

We have a high value for setting our interns up for success in every area of their lives. We have found a personal growth list to be helpful in giving them a well-rounded experience and preparing them for life after internship.

In addition to individual goals you will determine with your mentor, please complete the following throughout your internship. Write down what you learn from these experiences, pay attention to revelations you receive, and be ready to share highlights. We will discuss these as a team periodically during the year.

- Listen to two hours of Dave Ramsey's financial management podcast (you can find it on his website)
- Listen to 30 separate "Minute with Maxwell" sessions
- Read the entire New Testament

- Read Proverbs
- Prepare an hour-long teaching/ministry time for church leadership class students
- Send Steve and Melissa links to three websites that have great teaching on time/life management
- Participate in our group reading of Steve's books, and be ready to share a quote from the books at each intern meeting (be aware we might not always ask for a quote)
- Do three specific things to improve your physical health (e.g., read a book on nutrition, start an exercise program, read an article on the benefits of drinking water, etc.)
- Visit the Worship Rooms once
- Visit the Prayer chapel three times
- Go on a prayer drive/walk in Redding two times
- Visit a local tourist area you've never been to

WEEKLY GOAL SETTING EMAILS FROM INTERN TO MENTOR

This is one of the most important ways to stay connected with interns. We suggest not doing this if you cannot respond to these emails each week.

Here is an example of the format we prefer for weekly goal-setting emails. We've included two emails so the format from week to week will be clear. Here are some guidelines we give our team:

- List "Goals for this week" in bullet points.
- When writing a subsequent email the following week, copy and paste the bullet points under "Goals for this week" into "Goals and hours for last week" so we can easily see how you did on meeting your goals.
- Make a note if something is done, progress is made, or if it is not done.
- List the time spent on each item under "Goals and hours last week."
- There may be some things that happen every week (such as meetings, emails, misc. admin, etc.) that live under "Goals and hours last week" and don't move back and forth.
- Include a weekly "High," "Low," and "Something you don't know about me yet" as we highly value this relational piece. These can be work related or personal.
- Please make the subject line of these emails "Weekly Email [insert dates]"
- Please send us your weekly emails by Monday at noon. They will be due each

week at this time, so please plan ahead if you are unable to write yours on Monday mornings.

SAMPLE EMAIL #1

Goals and hours last week:
- Meetings (Third Year meeting, Backlund Team intern meeting, one on one meeting with Steve, intern teaching time, Ignite meeting) – 7 hours (done)
- Church leadership class and student church service – 3 hours (done)
- Attend GL video conference – 1.5 hours (done)
- LDP Prophetic Words (compile, edit, and send) – 2.5 hours (done)
- Help at GL Booth – 1 hour (done)
- Personal growth – Listen to 2 hours of Dave Ramsey podcast (not done)
- Emails/misc. admin – 3 hours

Total hours: 18 hours

Goals for this week:
- Meetings (Third Year meeting, Backlund Team intern meeting, intern teaching time, GL intern meeting, project meeting)
- Church leadership class and student church service
- LDP Prophetic Words (compile, edit, and send)
- Fill out intern questionnaire
- Edit blogs
- Lead team meeting for upcoming ministry trip
- Personal growth – Listen to 2 hours of Dave Ramsey podcast

High: Have them share the best moment of the past week, related to internship or not (e.g., I had a life-changing encounter with God regarding the season I'm in).
Low: Have them share the most challenging moment of the past week, related to internship or not (e.g., I didn't sleep well last week so I'm not feeling rested).
Something you don't know about me yet: This is a fun one Melissa started because she has had quite an adventurous life and wanted to find a consistent way to share something new with Steve – we have made it part of both our staff and intern weekly emails (e.g., I used to be a firefighter and especially enjoyed driving the fire engine and doing high-angle rope rescue).

SAMPLE EMAIL #2:

Goals and hours last week:

- Meetings (Third Year meeting, Backlund Team intern meeting, intern teaching time, GL intern meeting, project meeting) – 6.5 hours (done)
- Church leadership class and student church service – 3 hours (done)
- LDP Prophetic Words (compile, edit, and send) – 2 hours (done)
- Fill out intern questionnaire – 30 minutes (done)
- Edit blogs – 1 hour (done)
- Lead team meeting for upcoming ministry trip – 1.5 hours (done)
- Personal growth: Listen to 2 hours of Dave Ramsey podcast – 2 hours (done)
- Emails/misc. admin – 2.5 hours

Total hours: 19 hours

Goals for this week:
- Meetings (Third Year meeting, Backlund Team intern meeting, intern teaching time, meet with Melissa)
- Church leadership class and student church service
- Prep for ministry trip
- Go on ministry trip with Steve
- Personal growth – read Proverbs

High: I went to Burney Falls with friends and it was beautiful!
Low: I need some financial breakthrough.
Something you don't know about me yet: I won a dance competition on an Alaskan cruise while I was blindfolded (the dance was the Electric Slide). They showed it on the Cruise TV channel throughout the rest of the week.

INTERN QUESTIONNAIRE

We give our interns an online questionnaire to fill in at the beginning of the intern year. Daniel Newton, who runs a discipleship housing program called Grace Place, gave the idea to us. He created an information survey that's worded in a way that it's not obvious Daniel is looking for ways to bless the people in his houses – he is big on surprise. It can be tailored to suit your needs. The Backlund team version below is different from the original as our purpose is different. We want to bless people on our team, but we aren't trying to surprise them. We also give everyone on our team access to the results to help them get to know each other and to see practical ways to bless each other.

Basic information:
> Full Name:
> Spouse and children's names (if applicable):
> Birth date:
> Hometown:

Favorites list:
> Favorite candy bar available in US:
> Favorite snack:
> Favorite drink at Starbucks:
> Favorite ice cream flavor (or alternative if you don't eat dairy):
> Favorite place to get a gift card from:
> Favorite book of the Bible:
> Favorite person of the Bible (other than God/Jesus):
> Favorite Bible verse:
> Favorite hobbies:
> Favorite sport to play:
> Favorite sport to watch:
> Favorite sports team:
> Favorite board game:
> Favorite quote:

Getting to know you:
> Describe your ideal day off:
> Name a place you haven't visited near Redding that you'd like to see/explore:
> What is something unique about you?
> What are you most passionate about?
> List five things that make you feel valued or loved:
> List five things that don't make you feel valued or loved:
> What are your top love languages to give and receive? (These sometimes differ.)
> What are your DISC profile results? (You can take a free online version if you don't know.)

QUESTIONS FOR ONE ON ONE INTERN MEETINGS

We like to email our interns three to four questions that we will discuss in our next one on one meeting with them. It's best to email these ahead of time so they have time to process their answers. We also ask them to email us any topics they would like to discuss in their next meeting and any questions they have for us. This helps the mentor and the intern be prepared for meetings. We may discuss other things as well, but this creates a great starting point. Here are some sample questions to get you started (and we recommend rotating questions):

- What are some areas you feel like you're doing well in?
- What areas have been challenging?
- What are you doing for personal growth?
- What is standing out to you from the Backlund's message?
- What have you been learning from Bethel services recently? Which service do you regularly attend?
- What other books/teachings are you reading/listening to lately?
- Have you traveled with Steve recently? If so, what were the highlights? What's one thing that could be improved?
- What are you enjoying about Steve's Church Leadership class? Do you have a suggestion for how to upgrade it?
- How has your student-led church service experience been? What has been going well? What has been challenging?
- Are there specific things you'd like to discuss or questions you would like to ask in your upcoming one on one?
- How do you feel you are doing with relating to the rest of the intern team?
- Do you feel you have been fully bringing yourself to the table? Please explain.
- What has God been teaching you lately?
- What season do you feel like you're in? What is the theme or focus for you in this season?
- What are three goals you have for your internship?
- What is your plan to fulfill each of these goals?
- What are your plans for after graduation?
- What does a successful internship look like to you?
- Is there a way that Steve and/or Melissa can help improve your intern experience?
- What are your dreams for after internship?
- What steps can you take now toward these dreams?
- What's a success you've had in your life that you would love to see repeated?
- What are some areas in which you've had breakthrough that you'd like to see others do well in?
- Where do you see yourself 10 years from now? How about in 20 years?
- What do you want to be remembered for?
- What is the impact you most want to leave on the world?

Appendix D

Empowering Staff Appraisal

This is the annual appraisal we use with our Igniting Hope employees.

Here is the process for your annual appraisal:

1. You do a self-evaluation before your appointment with me in January.
2. At your January appointment, we will go over your self-evaluation, and I will give you my input on what is going well and any needed areas for improvement.

Self-evaluation – please put the following areas of job performance in order from what you believe is your strongest to what you believe is your weakest:

- Hunger to get Wendy's and Steve's message in your life
- Courteousness and excellence in how you represent Igniting Hope in emails, personal interactions, and phone conversations you have with people
- Following through on what you say you will do
- Setting goals for upcoming schedule and following through on goals
- Being a self-starter
- Managing your time well
- Finding better ways to do your job
- Delegating your duties to your team
- Giving feedback to Steve or Wendy on challenges within your job
- Proactivity in anticipating what is ahead
- Anticipating and understanding Steve's (or Wendy's) needs for information and for needs they have (and then addressing those)

- Bethel core values operating in your life
- Working and communicating with our intern team and fellow staff
- Determining and following through on professional training/goals related to your job

Appendix E

Grace Place:
The Culture of Empowerment in Action

Nine years ago, Daniel Newton was asked to oversee a house of male BSSM students. What started out as very basic housing has turned into a multi-house discipleship program called Grace Place that serves students in all three years of BSSM and gives them a housing option that includes community, accountability, covering, opportunities to be empowered, worship nights, preaching experience, and so much more. The vision is to enhance growth while in BSSM and to give the students opportunities they don't get elsewhere. (See www.graceplaceredding.com for further information.)

Here are a few of the ways Daniel has created a culture of empowerment within Grace Place:

- The houses have family nights in which they learn about grace, identity, and the cross (Jesus and the cross are main theme and that Grace Place focuses on).
- During family nights, the students have dinner, share their lows and highs, have corporate worship, and Daniel or a guest (often a Bethel leader) preaches.
- They have beginning and end of the year retreats to build connection. At the beginning of the year retreat, they bring sleeping bags and don't know what they're coming into. On their beds is their favorite candy bar, chips, drink, a welcome card, cardstock booklet of prophetic words from 49 people, and toiletries (like at a hotel).
- Daniel implements event nights focusing on prophesy, worship, evangelism,

preaching (the students prepare messages and preach for 10-12 minutes on Grace Place core values and various scriptures and themes), and/or fun events (shooting, paintballing, day trips, etc.).

- He wants people who are focused and who want to grow, be discipled, and are positioned as sons/daughters, so he denies about 60% of applicants.

- In the beginning of the year, Daniel creates a pictorial directory so the students in all the houses can learn to recognize each other and also go through the directory and write out a word for each person (about 50 words), which is given to them at the beginning of the year retreat.

- The First and Second Year programs are quite different (although they share the weekly family night and monthly event in common) to best suit the needs of the students.

- Some questions discussed at family night would be: What are three things I did well this week? What's one thing I can improve on? What did I learn from family night?

- The Second Year students go to the First Year houses and coach the First Year students. They have one on ones monthly and go to the house of the students they are coaching at least weekly.

- His internship is for people who have been through the program and the interns oversee a house.

- Daniel is not after numbers when it comes to students – essentially he wants to be intentional about quality time and interactions.

- The big core values at Grace Place are intentionality (looking for ways to love, serve, and honor people) and excellence.

- Grace Place has a healthy confrontational culture because confrontation comes easy when you know you're loved.

- Daniel is very big on believing in people before they believe in themselves and empowering people before they deserve it to exemplify and extend grace.

- He is also intentional about teaching the Grace Place residents how to use gifts for selfless reasons, not selfish reasons. Love is not self-seeking. It's about giving, not receiving. For example, many use the results of the love language test for themselves to learn how to get, not how to give. Love languages are intended to show us how we can better love others, not to put a demand on others of how to love us.

- The information survey Daniel developed is used to bless incoming students throughout the year – he leaves treats on their beds during retreat as mentioned, and he also blesses them on their birthdays, and other times throughout the year.

Appendix F

Ten Keys to Lessen Team Relationship Challenges:

1. Communicate proactively
2. Have clear and agreed upon expectations
3. Have clear job descriptions and adequate training
4. Give authority with responsibility
5. Have the same or very similar core values
6. Have regular team member reviews
7. Have strategies in place to quickly detect frustration
8. Reward excellence and high achievers
9. Pursue disgruntled people at earliest time
10. Be clear in defining the relationship

ADDITIONAL RESOURCES FROM STEVE & WENDY

VICTORIOUS MINDSETS

What we believe is ultimately more important than what we do. The course of our lives is set by our deepest core beliefs. Our mindsets are either a stronghold for God's purposes or a playhouse for the enemy. In this book, fifty biblical attitudes are revealed that are foundational for those who desire to walk in freedom and power.

CRACKS IN THE FOUNDATION

Going to a higher level in establishing key beliefs will affect ones intimacy with God and fruitfulness for the days ahead. This book challenges many basic assumptions of familiar Bible verses and common Christian phrases that block numerous benefits of our salvation. The truths shared in this book will help fill and repair "cracks" in our thinking which rob us of our God-given potential.

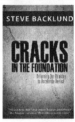

YOU'RE CRAZY IF YOU DON'T TALK TO YOURSELF

Jesus did not just think His way out of the wilderness and neither can we. He spoke truth to invisible beings and mindsets that sought to restrict and defeat Him. This book reveals that life and death are truly in the power of the tongue, and emphasize the necessity of speaking truth to our souls. Our words really do set the course of our lives and the lives of others (Proverbs 18:21, James 3:2-5).

LET'S JUST LAUGH AT THAT

Our hope level is an indicator of whether we are believing truth or lies. Truth creates hope and freedom, but believing lies brings hopelessness and restriction. We can have great theology but still be powerless because of deception about the key issues of life. Many of these self-defeating mindsets exist in our subconscious and have never been identified. This book exposes numerous falsehoods and reveals truth that makes us free. Get ready for a joy-infused adventure into hope-filled living.

LIVING FROM THE UNSEEN

This book will help you identify beliefs that block the reception of God's blessings and hinder our ability to live out our destiny. This book reveals that 1) Believing differently, not trying harder, is the key to change; 2) You cannot do what you don't believe you are; 3) You can only receive what you think you are worth; 4) Rather than learning how to die — it is time to learn how to live.

DIVINE STRATEGIES FOR INCREASE

The laws of the spirit are more real than the natural laws. God's laws are primarily principles to release blessing, not rules to be obeyed to gain right standing with God. The Psalmist talks of one whose greatest delight is in the law of the Lord. This delight allows one to discover new aspects of the nature of God (hidden in each law) to behold and worship. The end result of this delighting is a transformed life that prospers in every endeavor. His experience can be our experience, and this book unlocks the blessings hidden in the spiritual realm.

POSSESSING JOY

In His presence is fullness of joy (Psalm 16:11). Joy is to increase as we go deeper in our relationship with God. Religious tradition has devalued the role that gladness and laughter have for personal victory and kingdom advancement. His presence may not always produce joy; but if we never or rarely have fullness of joy, we must reevaluate our concept of God. This book takes one on a journey toward the headwaters of the full joy that Jesus often spoke of. Get ready for joy to increase and strength and longevity to ignite.

IGNITING FAITH IN 40 DAYS

There must be special seasons in our lives when we break out of routine and do something that will ignite our faith about God and our identity in Christ. This book will lead you through the life-changing experience of a 40-day negativity fast. This fast teaches the power of declaring truth and other transforming daily customs that will strengthen your foundation of faith and radically increase your personal hope.

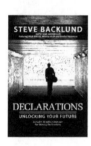

DECLARATIONS

"Nothing happens in the kingdom unless a declaration is made." Believers everywhere are realizing the power of declarations to empower their lives. You may be wondering, "What are declarations and why are people making them?" or maybe, "Aren't declarations simply a repackaged 'name it and claim' heresy?" Declarations answers these questions by sharing 30 biblical reasons for declaring truth over every area of life. Steve Backlund and his team also answer common objections and concerns to the teaching about declarations. The revelation this book carries will help you to set the direction your life will go. Get ready for 30 days of powerful devotions and declarations that will convince you that life is truly in the power of the tongue.

CRUCIAL MOMENTS

This book helps us upgrade how we think, act, and most importantly, believe in those crucial moments when: You feel nervous about speaking in public, Your house is a mess when people come over, A politician whose beliefs oppose yours is elected, You gain more weight than you thought, You don't feel like worshipping and 47 other opportunities for breakthrough.

HELP! I'M A PASTOR

This book is practical, revelatory, and humorous, with 50 common scenarios that could cause a pastor to say, "They didn't prepare me for this in Bible school!" *HELP! I'm A Pastor* replaces exasperation with expectation using 80 life and leadership core values to tackle situations including: My People Are Always Late For Meetings, I Am Tempted To Have An Affair, How Transparent Is Too Transparent?, and Pastor, She Is A Jezebel.

LET'S JUST LAUGH AT THAT FOR KIDS!

We all want the best for the young people in our lives. "Let's Just Laugh at That for Kids!" will help you set children up for success by teaching them to replace lies with truth and to take a combative stance against beliefs that try to hold them back. This book invites you into an interactive journey in taking every thought captive with the kids you love. Through these fun, laughter–filled pages, we expose twenty common lies kids often believe, and this book helps train them to use "laughter weapons" to disarm the lies. We then use Scripture, declarations, and practical wisdom to reinforce the truth.

Audio message series are available through the Igniting Hope store at: IgnitingHope.com
All books available on Kindle at Amazon.com

Made in the USA
Charleston, SC
03 November 2016